first published 1985

© William Collins Sons & Co. Ltd. 1985

Latest reprint 1993

ISBN 0 00 459335 9

Printed in Great Britain by
HarperCollins Manufacturing, Glasgow

This book has been designed to help all learners of German to get to grips with the grammar of the language, whatever stage you are in learning German. For beginners, the book provides a clear introduction to all the basic rules and structures, and more advanced learners will find it an invaluable guide for reference and revision.

For ease of use, each part of speech (nouns, verbs, adjectives etc) has been treated separately (see the list of contents on the next page). Wherever we think a grammatical term may be unfamiliar this has been explained or illustrated at the appropriate point in the text.

A special feature of this compact book is the clear demarcation of grammatical points, each treated on a left-hand page, and illustrated by examples in up-to-date German on the opposite right-hand page. The eye is guided instantly to the appropriate example(s) by a system of bracketed numbers, e.g. (→1), (→2) etc, corresponding to an example number on the facing page. This means a clear, uncluttered presentation of the grammatical points, while allowing plenty of space for illustrating them.

Particular attention is paid throughout to those areas where German usage differs from English, thus helping the user to avoid the pitfalls of translating English structures by identical structures in German. Further sections at the back of the book give guidance in the use of numbers, and an area where German is very different from English: punctuation.

A fully comprehensive index, listing key words in both English and German, as well as grammatical references, completes the book.

Abbreviations used

acc.	accusative	gen.	genitive
ctd.	continued	masc.	masculine
dat.	dative	neut.	neuter
fem.	feminine	nom.	nominative
ff.	and following pages	p(p).	page(s)

4 CONTENTS

Tense Formation

Tenses are either **simple** or **compound**. Once you know how to form the past participle, compound tenses are similar for all verbs (see pp.22 to 29). To form simple tenses you need to know whether a verb is **weak**, **strong** or **mixed**.

Simple Tenses

In German these are:

Present indicative   (→**1**)
Imperfect indicative   (→**2**)
Present subjunctive   (→**3**)
Imperfect subjunctive   (→**4**)

Subjunctive forms are widely used in German, especially for indirect or reported speech (see pp.66 and 67).

The simple tenses are formed by adding endings to a verb **stem**. The endings show the number, person and tense of the subject of the verb (→**5**)

The types of verb you need to know to form simple tenses are:

● **Strong verbs** (pp.12 to 15), those whose vowel usually changes in forming the imperfect indicative (→**6**)

● **Weak verbs** (pp.8 to 11), which are usually completely regular and have no vowel changes. Their endings differ from those of strong verbs (→**7**)

● **Mixed verbs** (pp.16 and 17), which have a vowel change like strong verbs, but the endings of weak verbs (→**8**)

Continued

1 ich hole
I fetch, I am fetching, I do fetch

2 ich holte
I fetched, I was fetching, I used to fetch

3 (daß) ich hole
(that) I fetch/I fetched

4 (daß) ich holte
(that) I fetched

5 ich hole	I fetch
wir holen	we fetch
du holtest	you fetched

6 singen	to sing
er singt	he sings
er sang	he sang

7 holen	to fetch
er holt	he fetches
er holte	he fetched

8 nennen	to name
er nennt	he names
er nannte	he named

Weak Verbs

Weak verbs are usually **regular** in conjugation. Their simple tenses are formed as follows:

- **Present** and **imperfect** tenses are formed by adding the endings shown below to the verb **stem**. This stem is formed by removing the **-en** ending of the infinitive (the form found in the dictionary) (→1)

- Where the infinitive of a weak verb ends in **-eln** or **-ern**, only the **-n** is removed to form the verb stem (→2)

- The endings are as follows (→3):

	PRESENT INDICATIVE	PRESENT SUBJUNCTIVE
1st. singular	-e	-e
2nd.	-st	-est
3rd.	-t	-e
1st. plural	-en	-en
2nd.	-t	-et
3rd.	-en	-en

	IMPERFECT INDICATIVE	IMPERFECT SUBJUNCTIVE
1st. singular	-te	-te
2nd.	-test	-test
3rd.	-te	-te
1st. plural	-ten	-ten
2nd.	-tet	-tet
3rd.	-ten	-ten

Continued

1 INFINITIVE   STEM
  holen   to fetch   **hol-**
  machen   to make   **mach-**
  kauen   to chew   **kau-**

2 **wandern**   to roam   **wander-**
  handeln   to trade,   **handel-**
               to act

3 **holen**   to fetch

PRESENT INDICATIVE	PRESENT SUBJUNCTIVE	
ich hole	ich hole	I fetch
du holst	du holest	you fetch
er/sie/es holt	er/sie/es hole	he/she/it fetches
wir holen	wir holen	we fetch
ihr holt	ihr holet	you (*plural*) fetch
sie/Sie holen	sie/Sie holen	they/you (*polite*) fetch

IMPERFECT INDICATIVE AND SUBJUNCTIVE
(*These tenses are identical for weak verbs*)

ich holte	I fetched
du holtest	you fetched
er/sie/es holte	he/she/it fetched
wir holten	we fetched
ihr holtet	you (*plural*) fetched
sie/Sie holten	they/you (*polite*) fetched

Weak Verbs (ctd.)

- Where the stem of a weak verb ends in **-d** or **-t**, an extra **-e-** is inserted before those endings where this will ease pronunciation (→**1**)

- Weak verbs whose stems end in **-m** or **-n** may take this extra **-e-**, or not, depending on whether its addition is necessary for pronunciation. If the **-m** or **-n** is preceded by a consonant *other than* **l**, **r** or **h**, the **-e-** is inserted (→**2**)

- Weak (and strong) verbs whose stem ends in a sibilant sound (**-s**, **-z**, **-ß**) normally lose the **-s** of the second person singular ending (the **du** form) in the present indicative (→**3**)

  NOTE: When this sibilant is **-sch**, the **-s-** of the ending remains (→**4**)

1 reden to speak

PRESENT	IMPERFECT
ich rede	ich redete
du redest	du redetest
er redet	er redete
wir reden	wir redeten
ihr redet	ihr redetet
sie reden	sie redeten

arbeiten to work

PRESENT	IMPERFECT
ich arbeite	ich arbeitete
du arbeitest	du arbeitetest
er arbeitet	er arbeitete
wir arbeiten	wir arbeiteten
ihr arbeitet	ihr arbeitetet
sie arbeiten	sie arbeiteten

2 atmen to breathe

PRESENT	IMPERFECT
ich atme	ich atmete
du atmest	du atmetest
er atmet	er atmete
wir atmen	wir atmeten
ihr atmet	ihr atmetet
sie atmen	sie atmeten

segnen to bless

PRESENT	IMPERFECT
ich segne	ich segnete
du segnest	du segnetest
er segnet	er segnete
wir segnen	wir segneten
ihr segnet	ihr segnetet
sie segnen	sie segneten

BUT:

umarmen to embrace

ich umarme	ich umarmte
du umarmst	du umarmtest
er umarmt	er umarmte
wir umarmen	wir umarmten
ihr umarmt	ihr umarmtet
sie umarmen	sie umarmten

lernen to learn

ich lerne	ich lernte
du lernst	du lerntest
er lernt	er lernte
wir lernen	wir lernten
ihr lernt	ihr lerntet
sie lernen	sie lernten

3 grüßen to greet

PRESENT
ich grüße
du grüßt
er grüßt
wir grüßen
ihr grüßt
sie grüßen

4 löschen to extinguish

PRESENT
ich lösche
du löschst
er löscht
wir löschen
ihr löscht
sie löschen

Strong Verbs

A list of the most useful strong verbs is given on pp.86 to 97.

● What differentiates strong verbs from weak ones is that when forming their **imperfect indicative** tense, strong verbs undergo a vowel change and have a different set of endings (→1)

 Their past participles are also formed differently (see p.24).

● To form the **imperfect subjunctive** of strong verbs, the endings from the appropriate table below are added to the stem of the imperfect indicative, but the vowel is modified by an umlaut where this is possible, i.e. **a → ä, o → ö, u → ü**. Exceptions to this are clearly shown in the table of strong verbs (→2)

The endings for the simple tenses of strong verbs are as follows (→3)

	PRESENT INDICATIVE	PRESENT SUBJUNCTIVE
1st. singular	-e	-e
2nd.	-st	-est
3rd.	-t	-e
1st. plural	-en	-en
2nd.	-t	-et
3rd.	-en	-en

	IMPERFECT INDICATIVE	IMPERFECT SUBJUNCTIVE
1st. singular	—	-e
2nd.	-st	-(e)st
3rd.	—	-e
1st. plural	-en	-en
2nd.	-t	-(e)t
3rd.	-en	-en

Continued

1 Compare:

	INFINITIVE	PRESENT	IMPERFECT
WEAK	**sagen** to say	**er sagt**	**er sagte**
STRONG	**rufen** to shout	**er ruft**	**er rief**

2

	IMPERFECT INDICATIVE	IMPERFECT SUBJUNCTIVE
	er gab he gave	**er gäbe** (*umlaut added*)
BUT	**er rief** he shouted	**er riefe** (*no umlaut possible*)

3 **singen** to sing

PRESENT INDICATIVE	PRESENT SUBJUNCTIVE
ich singe	ich singe
du singst	du singest
er singt	er singe
wir singen	wir singen
ihr singt	ihr singet
sie singen	sie singen
Sie singen	Sie singen

IMPERFECT INDICATIVE	IMPERFECT SUBJUNCTIVE
ich sang	ich sänge
du sangst	du säng(e)st
er sang	er sänge
wir sangen	wir sängen
ihr sangt	ihr säng(e)t
sie sangen	sie sängen
Sie sangen	Sie sängen

Strong Verbs (ctd.)

● In the present tense of strong verbs, the vowel also often changes for the second and third persons singular (the **du** and **er/sie/es** forms).
The pattern of possible changes is as follows:

long **e** → **ie**
short **e** → **i**
a → **ä**
au → **äu**
o → **ö**

Verbs which undergo these changes are clearly shown in the table on p.86 (→**1**)

● Strong (and weak) verbs whose stem ends with a sibilant sound (**-s**, **-z**, **-ß**) normally lose the **-s** of the second person singular ending (the **du** form) in the *present indicative*, unless the sibilant is **-sch**, when it remains (→**2**)

● In the second person singular of the *imperfect* tense of strong verbs whose stem ends in a sibilant sound (including **-sch**) the sibilant remains, and an **-e-** is inserted between it and the appropriate ending (→**3**)

1 **sehen** to see
ich sehe
du siehst
er/sie/es sieht
wir sehen
ihr seht
sie sehen

helfen to help
ich helfe
du hilfst
er/sie/es hilft
wir helfen
ihr helft
sie helfen

fahren to drive
ich fahre
du fährst
er fährt
wir fahren
ihr fahrt
sie fahren

saufen to booze
ich saufe
du säufst
er säuft
wir saufen
ihr sauft
sie saufen

stoßen to push
ich stoße
du stößt
er stößt
wir stoßen
ihr stoßt
sie stoßen

2 **wachsen** to grow
ich wachse
du wächst
er wächst
wir wachsen
ihr wachst
sie wachsen

waschen to wash
ich wasche
du wäschst
er wäscht
wir waschen
ihr wascht
sie waschen

3 **lesen** to read
ich las
du lasest
er las
wir lasen
ihr last
sie lasen

schließen to close
ich schloß
du schlossest
er schloß
wir schlossen
ihr schloßt
sie schlossen

waschen to wash
ich wusch
du wuschest
er wusch
wir wuschen
ihr wuscht
sie wuschen

Mixed Verbs

There are nine **mixed** verbs in German, and, as their name implies, they are formed according to a mixture of the rules already outlined for weak and strong verbs.

The mixed verbs are:

denken to think	**kennen** to know	**nennen** to name
rennen to run	**senden** to send	**bringen** to bring
brennen to burn	**wenden** to turn	**wissen** to know

Full details of their principal parts are given in the verb list beginning on p.86.

- Mixed verbs form their **imperfect** tense by adding the weak verb endings to a stem whose vowel has been changed as for a strong verb (→**1**)

  NOTE: **bringen** and **denken** have a consonant change too in their imperfect forms (→**2**)

- The **imperfect subjunctive** forms of mixed verbs are unusual and should be noted (→**3**)

- Other tenses of mixed verbs are formed as for strong verbs.

- The past participle of mixed verbs has characteristics of both weak and strong verbs, as shown on p.24.

1 IMPERFECT INDICATIVE

kennen to know	**wissen** to know	**senden** to send
ich kannte	ich wußte	ich sandte
du kanntest	du wußtest	du sandtest
er kannte	er wußte	er sandte
wir kannten	wir wußten	wir sandten
ihr kanntet	ihr wußtet	ihr sandtet
sie kannten	sie wußten	sie sandten

2 IMPERFECT INDICATIVE

denken to think	**bringen** to bring
ich dachte	ich brachte
du dachtest	du brachtest
er dachte	er brachte
wir dachten	wir brachten
ihr dachtet	ihr brachtet
sie dachten	sie brachten

3 IMPERFECT SUBJUNCTIVE

kennen	**rennen**	**senden**
ich kennte	ich rennte	ich sendete
du kenntest	du renntest	du sendetest
er kennte *etc*	er rennte *etc*	er sendete *etc*

brennen	**wissen**	**wenden**
ich brennte	ich wüßte	ich wendete
du brenntest	du wüßtest	du wendetest
er brennte *etc*	er wüßte *etc*	er wendete *etc*

denken	**bringen**	**nennen**
ich dächte	ich brächte	ich nennte
du dächtest	du brächtest	du nenntest
er dächte *etc*	er brächte *etc*	er nennte *etc*

The Imperative

This is the form of a verb used to give an order or a command, or to make a request:

> *Come here/stand up/please bring me a beer*   (→1)

- German has three main imperative forms. These go with the three ways of addressing people **Sie, du** and **ihr** (see p.160)

	FORMATION	EXAMPLES	
SINGULAR	stem(+e)	**hol(e)!**	*fetch!*
PLURAL	stem+t	**holt!**	*fetch!*
POLITE (*sing* and *pl*)	stem+**en Sie**	**holen Sie!**	*fetch!*

- The **-e** of the singular form is often dropped, BUT NOT where the verb stem ends in **-t, -d, -chn, -ckn, -dn, -fn, -gn** or **-tm**   (→2)

- **Weak verbs** ending in **-eln** or **-ern** take the **-e** ending in the singular form, but the additional **-e-** within the stem may be dropped   (→3)

- Any vowel change in the present tense of a **strong verb** (see p.14) occurs also in its singular imperative form and no **-e** is added   (→4)

  BUT if the vowel modification in the present tense of a **strong verb** is the addition of an umlaut, this is not added in the singular form of the imperative   (→5)

- In the imperative form of a **reflexive verb** (see p.30) the pronoun is placed immediately after the verb   (→6)

- **Separable prefixes** (see p.72) are placed at the end of an imperative statement   (→7)

Continued

1 SINGULAR: **Komm mal her!**   Come here!
  PLURAL: **Steht auf!**   Stand up!
  POLITE: **Kommen Sie herein**   Do come in

2 **Hör zu!** Listen
  Hol es! Fetch it
  BUT:
  Arbeite tüchtig! Work hard

3 **wandern**   to walk   **handeln**   to act
  wand(e)re!   walk!   **hand(e)le!**   act!

4 **nehmen**   to take   **helfen**   to help
  du nimmst   you take   **du hilfst**   you help
  nimm!   take!   **hilf!**   help!

  EXCEPTION:
  sehen   to see
  sieh(e)!   see!

5 **laufen**   to run   **stoßen**   to push
  du läufst   you run   **du stößt**   you push
  lauf(e)!   run!   **stoß(e)!**   push!

6 **sich setzen** to sit down:
  setz dich!
  setzt euch!
  setzen Sie sich!

7 **zumachen** to close: **aufhören** to stop:
  Mach die Tür zu!   **Hör aber endlich auf!**
  Close the door!   Do stop it!

The Imperative (ctd.)

- Imperatives are followed in German by an exclamation mark, unless the imperative is not intended as a command (→1)

- **du** and **ihr**, though not normally present in imperative forms, may be included for emphasis (→2)

- An imperative form also exists for the **wir** form of the verb. It consists of the normal present tense form, but with the pronoun **wir** *following* the verb. It is used for making suggestions (→3)

- The imperative forms of **sein** (*to be*) are irregular (→4)

- The particles **auch, nur, mal, doch** are frequently used with imperatives. They heighten or soften the imperative effect, or add a note of encouragement to a request or command. Often they have no direct equivalent in English and are therefore not always translated (→5)

Some Alternatives to the Imperative in German

- Infinitives are often used instead of the imperative in written instructions or public announcements (→6)

- The impersonal passive (see p.34) may be used (→7)

- Nouns, adjectives or adverbs can also be used with imperative effect (→8)
  Some of these have become set expressions (→9)

1 Laß ihn in Ruhe! Leave him alone
   Sagen Sie mir bitte, wie spät es ist
   What's the time please?

2 Geht ihr voran! You go on ahead
   Sag du ihm, was los ist You tell him what's wrong

3 Nehmen wir an also, daß ...
   Let's assume then that ...
   Sagen wir mal, es habe 4.000 DM gekostet
   Let's just say it cost 4,000 marks

4 sein to be
   sei!
   seid!
   seien wir!
   seien Sie!

5 Geh doch! Go on!/Get going!
   Sag mal, ... Tell me ...
   Versuchen Sie es mal! Do give it a try!
   Komm schon! Do come/Please come
   Mach es auch richtig! Be sure to do it properly

6 Einsteigen!
   All aboard!
   Zwiebeln abziehen und in Ringe schneiden
   Peel the onions and slice them

7 Jetzt wird aufgeräumt!
   You're going to clear up now!

8 Ruhe! Be quiet! Silence!
   Vorsicht! Careful! Look out!

9 Achtung! Listen!/Attention!
   Rauchen verboten! No smoking

Compound Tenses

The present and imperfect tenses in German are **simple** tenses, as described on pp.6 to 17.

All other tenses, called **compound tenses,** are formed for all types of verb by using the appropriate tense of an **auxiliary verb** plus a part of the main verb.

There are three auxiliary verbs:
>   **haben** for past tenses
>   **sein** also for past tenses
>   **werden** for future and conditional tenses

The **compound past tenses** in German are:

Perfect indicative	(→1)
Perfect subjunctive	(→2)
Pluperfect indicative	(→3)
Pluperfect subjunctive	(→4)

These are dealt with on pp.26 ff.

The **future** and **conditional tenses** in German are all compound tenses. They are:

Future indicative	(→5)
Future subjunctive	(→6)
Future perfect	(→7)
Conditional	(→8)
Conditional perfect	(→9)

These are dealt with on pp.28 ff.

with **haben**	with **sein**

1 er hat geholt
he (has) fetched

er ist gereist
he (has) travelled

2 er habe geholt
he (has) fetched

er sei gereist
he (has) travelled

3 er hatte geholt
he had fetched

er war gereist
he had travelled

4 er hätte geholt
he had fetched

er wäre gereist
he had travelled

5 er wird holen
he will fetch

er wird reisen
he will travel

6 er werde holen
he will fetch

er werde reisen
he will travel

7 er wird geholt haben
he will have fetched

er wird gereist sein
he will have travelled

8 er würde holen
he would fetch

er würde reisen
he would travel

9 er würde geholt haben
he would have fetched

er würde gereist sein
he would have travelled

Compound Past Tenses: Formation

- Compound past tenses are normally formed by using the auxiliary verb **haben**, plus the past participle of the main verb (see below) (→**1**)

- Certain types of verb take **sein** instead of **haben**, and this is clearly indicated in the verb tables starting on p.86. They fall into three main types:
  1. intransitive verbs (those that take no direct object, often showing a change of state or place) (→**2**)
  2. certain verbs meaning "to happen" (→**3**)
  3. miscellaneous others, including:
     bleiben to remain, **gelingen** to succeed
     begegnen to meet, **sein** to be
     werden to become (→**4**)

- In some cases the verb can be conjugated with either **haben** or **sein**, depending on whether it is used transitively (with a direct object) or intransitively (where no direct object is possible) (→**5**)

The Past Participle: Formation (see also p.50)

- **Weak** verbs add the prefix **ge-** and the suffix **-t** to the verb stem (→**6**)
  Verbs ending in **-ieren** or **-eien** omit the **ge-** (→**7**)

- **Strong** verbs add the prefix **ge-** and the suffix **-en** to the verb stem (→**8**). The vowel of the stem may be modified (see verb list, p.86) (→**9**)

- **Mixed** verbs add the prefix **ge-** and the "weak" suffix **-t** to the stem. The stem vowel is modified as for many strong verbs (→**10**)

Continued

1 Haben Sie gut geschlafen?
Did you sleep well?
Die Kinder hatten fleißig gearbeitet
The children had worked hard

2 Wir sind nach Bonn gefahren
We went to Bonn
Er ist schnell eingeschlafen
He quickly fell asleep

3 Was ist geschehen?
What happened?

4 Er ist zu Hause geblieben   **Er ist krank gewesen**
He stayed at home   He has been ill
Es ist uns nicht gelungen   **Sie ist krank geworden**
We did not succeed   She became ill
Er ist einem Freund begegnet
He met a friend

5 Er hat den Wagen nach Köln gefahren
He drove the car to Cologne
Er ist nach Köln gefahren
He went to Cologne

6 holen to fetch   **9 singen** to sing
geholt fetched   **gesungen** sung

7 studieren to study   **10 senden** to send
studiert studied   **gesandt** sent
prophezeien to prophesy   **bringen** to bring
prophezeit prophesied   **gebracht** brought

8 laufen to run
gelaufen ran

For a full list of strong and mixed verbs see p.86

Compound Past Tenses: Formation (ctd.)

The formation of past participles for weak, strong and mixed verbs is described on p.24, and a comprehensive list of the principle parts of the most commonly used strong and mixed verbs is provided for reference on pp.86 to 97.

How to form the compound past tenses:

Perfect indicative	the present tense of **haben** or **sein** plus the past participle of the verb (→1)
Perfect subjunctive	(used in indirect or reported speech) the present subjunctive of **haben** or **sein** plus the past participle (→2)
Pluperfect indicative	imperfect indicative of **haben** or **sein** plus the past participle (→3)
Pluperfect subjunctive	(for indirect or reported speech) imperfect subjunctive of **haben** or **sein** plus the past participle (→4)
	Note: The pluperfect subjunctive is a frequently used tense in German, since it can replace the much clumsier conditional perfect tense shown on p.28.

	with **haben**	with **sein**

1 PERFECT INDICATIVE

with **haben**	with **sein**
ich habe geholt	ich bin gereist
du hast geholt	du bist gereist
er/sie/es hat geholt	er/sie/es ist gereist
wir haben geholt	wir sind gereist
ihr habt geholt	ihr seid gereist
sie/Sie haben geholt	sie/Sie sind gereist

2 PERFECT SUBJUNCTIVE

with **haben**	with **sein**
ich habe geholt	ich sei gereist
du habest geholt	du sei(e)st gereist
er/sie/es habe geholt	er/sie/es sei gereist
wir haben geholt	wir seien gereist
ihr habet geholt	ihr seiet gereist
sie/Sie haben geholt	sie/Sie seien gereist

3 PLUPERFECT INDICATIVE

with **haben**	with **sein**
ich hatte geholt	ich war gereist
du hattest geholt	du warst gereist
er/sie/es hatte geholt	er/sie/es war gereist
wir hatten geholt	wir waren gereist
ihr hattet geholt	ihr wart gereist
sie/Sie hatten geholt	sie/Sie waren gereist

4 PLUPERFECT SUBJUNCTIVE

with **haben**	with **sein**
ich hätte geholt	ich wäre gereist
du hättest geholt	du wär(e)st gereist
er/sie/es hätte geholt	er/sie/es wäre gereist
wir hätten geholt	wir wären gereist
ihr hättet geholt	ihr wär(e)t gereist
sie/Sie hätten geholt	sie/Sie wären gereist

Future and Conditional Tenses: Formation

- The **future** and **conditional** tenses are formed in the same way for all verbs, whether weak, strong or mixed.

- The auxiliary **werden** is used for all verbs together with the infinitive of the main verb

- The infinitive is usually placed at the end of the clause (see p.224).

How to form the future and conditional tenses:

Future indicative
present tense of **werden** plus the infinitive of the verb (→1)

Future subjunctive
present subjunctive of **werden** plus the infinitive (→2)

Future perfect
present indicative of **werden** plus the **perfect infinitive** (see below) (→3)

Conditional
imperfect subjunctive of **werden** plus the infinitive (→4)

Conditional perfect
imperfect subjunctive of **werden** plus the perfect infinitive (see below) (→5)

Note: often replaced by the pluperfect subjunctive

- The **perfect infinitive** consists of the infinitive of **haben/sein** plus the past participle of the verb.

1 Du sollst dich sofort anziehen
  You are to get dressed immediately
2 Reg dich doch nicht so auf!
  Calm down!
3 Wir müssen uns beeilen
  We must hurry
4 Sie beschäftigen sich sehr mit den Kindern
  They spend a lot of time with the children
5 Hast du dich um diese Stelle beworben?
  Have you applied for this post?
6 Ich erinnere mich nicht daran
  I can't remember it
7 Ich freue mich auf die Fahrt
  I am looking forward to the journey
8 Interessiert du dich für Musik?
  Are you interested in music?
9 Er hat sich geirrt
  He was wrong
10 Bitte, setzt euch hin!
  Please sit down
11 Die Kinder sahen sich erstaunt um
  The children looked around in amazement

12 Eigentlich müßte man sich das Rauchen abgewöhnen
  One really ought to give up smoking
13 Bilde dir doch nichts ein!
  Don't kid yourself!
14 Eins könntest du dir doch erlauben
  You could surely allow yourself one
15 Wenn ich mir nur einen Mercedes leisten könnte!
  If only I could afford a Mercedes!
16 Du hast dir wieder zuviel vorgenommen!
  You've taken on too much again!
17 So hatte ich es mir oft vorgestellt
  I had often imagined it like this
18 Was wünscht ihr euch zu Weihnachten?
  What do you want for Christmas?

The Passive

In active tenses, the subject of a verb carries out the action of the verb, but in passive tenses the subject of the verb has something done to it.
Compare the following:

> *Peter kicked the cat* (subject: *Peter*)
> *The cat was kicked by Peter* (subject: *the cat*)

- English uses the verb "to be" to form its passive tenses. German uses **werden** (→1)
  A sample verb is conjugated in the passive on pp.39 to 41.

- In English, the word "by" usually introduces the agent through which the action of a passive tense is performed. In German this agent is introduced by:
  von for the performer of the action
  durch for an inanimate cause (→2)

- The passive can be used to add impersonality or distance to an event (→3)
  It may also be used where the identity of the cause of the deed is unknown or not important (→4)

- In general however the passive is used less in German than in English. The following are common replacements for the passive:

  1. an active tense with the impersonal pronoun **man** as subject (meaning *they/one*). This resembles the use of *on* in French, and **man** is not always translated as *one* or *they* (→5)

  2. **sich lassen** plus a verb in the infinitive (→6)

Continued

1 Das Auto wurde gekauft
The car was bought

2 Das ist von seinem Onkel geschickt worden
It was sent by his uncle
Das Kind wurde von einem Hund gebissen
The child was bitten by a dog
Seine Bewerbung ist von der Firma abgelehnt worden
(*the firm is viewed as a human agent*)
His application was turned down by the firm

Die Tür wurde durch den Wind geöffnet
The door was opened by the wind
Das Getreide wurde durch den Sturm niedergeschlagen
The crop was flattened by the storm

3 Die Praxis ist von Dr. Lehmann übernommen worden
The practice has been taken over by Dr Lehmann
Anfang 1767 wurde noch ein Anschlag auf sein Leben gemacht
Another attempt was made on his life early in 1767

4 In letzter Zeit sind neue Gesetze eingeführt worden
New laws have recently been introduced

5 Man hatte es schon verkauft
It had already been sold
Man wird es verkauft haben
It will have been sold

6 Das läßt sich schnell herausfinden
We'll/You'll/One will be able to find that out quickly

The Passive (ctd.)

- In English the indirect object of an active tense can become the subject of a passive statement. e.g.

    Peter gave *him* a car (*him* = to him)
    He was given a car by Peter

  This is not possible in German, where the indirect object (*him*) must remain in the dative case (see p. 110). There are two ways of handling this in German:
  1. with the direct object (*car*) as the subject of a passive verb (→1)
  2. by means of an impersonal passive construction, with or without the impersonal subject **es** (→1)

  These constructions would however normally be avoided in favour of an active tense, when the agent of the action is known (→2)

- Verbs which are normally followed by the dative case in German and so have only an indirect object (see p.80) should therefore be especially noted, as they can only adopt the impersonal or **man**-forms of the passive (→3)

- Some passive tenses are avoided in German, as they are inelegant (and difficult to use!). For instance, the future perfect passives should be replaced by an active tense or a **man**-construction (→4)

  The conditional perfect passives are also rarely used, past conditional being shown by the pluperfect subjunctives, either passive or active (→5)

- English passive constructions such as
  he was heard whistling/they were thought to be dying
  are not possible in German (→6)

Continued

1 Ein Auto wurde ihm von Peter gegeben
OR:
Es wurde ihm von Peter ein Auto gegeben
OR:
Ihm wurde von Peter ein Auto gegeben
He was given a car by Peter

2 Peter gab ihm ein Auto
Peter gave him a car

3 helfen (+ *dative*)   to help:

Sie half mir	**Mir wurde von ihr geholfen**
She helped me →	OR
	Es wurde mir von ihr geholfen
	I was helped by her

4 Er meint, es werde schon gesehen worden sein
He thinks that it will already have been seen

BETTER: **Er meint, man werde es schon gesehen haben**

5 Es würde geholt worden sein / Man würde es geholt haben
It would have been fetched

BETTER: **Es wäre geholt worden / Man hätte es geholt**

6 Man hörte ihn singen
He was heard singing
Man sah es ankommen
It was seen arriving
Man glaubte, er sei betrunken
He was thought to be drunk

Passive Tenses: Conjugation

Simple Tenses

Present passive indicative e.g. *it is seen*	present indicative of **werden** + past participle of the verb (→**1**)
Present passive subjunctive	present subjunctive of **werden** + past participle of the verb (→**2**)
Imperfect passive indicative e.g. *it was seen*	imperfect indicative of **werden** + past participle of the verb (→**3**)
Imperfect passive subjunctive	imperfect subjunctive of **werden** + past participle of the verb (→**4**)

Compound Tenses

Perfect passive indicative e.g. *it has been seen*	present indicative of **sein** + past participle of the verb + **worden** (→**5**)
Perfect passive subjunctive	present subjunctive of **sein** + past participle of the verb + **worden** (→**6**)
Pluperfect passive indicative e.g. *it had been seen*	imperfect indicative of **sein** + past participle + **worden** (→**7**)

Continued

1 PRESENT PASSIVE INDICATIVE
ich werde gesehen   **wir werden gesehen**
du wirst gesehen   **ihr werdet gesehen**
er/sie/es wird gesehen   **sie/Sie werden gesehen**

OR: **man sieht mich/man sieht dich** *etc*

2 PRESENT PASSIVE SUBJUNCTIVE
ich werde gesehen   **wir werden gesehen**
du werdest gesehen   **ihr werdet gesehen**
er/sie/es werde gesehen   **sie/Sie werden gesehen**

OR: **man sehe mich/man sehe dich** *etc*

3 IMPERFECT PASSIVE INDICATIVE
ich wurde gesehen/wir wurden gesehen *etc*

OR: **man sah mich/ man sah uns** *etc*

4 IMPERFECT PASSIVE SUBJUNCTIVE
ich würde gesehen/wir würden gesehen *etc*

OR: **man sähe mich/man sähe uns** *etc*

5 PERFECT PASSIVE INDICATIVE
ich bin gesehen worden/wir sind gesehen worden *etc*

OR: **man hat mich/uns gesehen** *etc*

6 PERFECT PASSIVE SUBJUNCTIVE
ich sei gesehen worden/wir seien gesehen worden *etc*

OR: **man habe mich/uns gesehen** *etc*

7 PLUPERFECT PASSIVE INDICATIVE
ich war gesehen worden/wir waren gesehen worden *etc*

OR: **man hatte mich/uns gesehen** *etc*

Passive Tenses: Conjugation (ctd.)

Pluperfect passive subjunctive	imperfect subjunctive of **sein** + past participle of the verb + **worden** (→1)
Present passive infinitive e.g. *it will be seen*	infinitive of **werden** + past participle of the verb (→2)
Future passive indicative e.g. *it will be seen*	present indicative of **werden** + present passive infinitive of the verb (→3)
Future passive subjunctive	present subjunctive of **werden** + present passive infinitive (→4)
Perfect passive infinitive e.g. *to have been seen*	past participle of the verb + **worden sein** (→5)
Future perfect passive e.g. *it will have been seen*	present indicative of **werden** + perfect passive infinitive of the verb (→6)
Conditional passive e.g. *it would be seen*	imperfect subjunctive of of **werden** + present passive infinitive of the verb (→7)
Conditional perfect passive e.g. *it would have been seen*	imperfect subjunctive of **werden** + perfect passive infinitive of the verb (→8)

1 PLUPERFECT PASSIVE SUBJUNCTIVE
ich wäre gesehen worden/wir wären gesehen worden *etc*

OR: **man hätte mich/uns gesehen** *etc*

2 PRESENT PASSIVE INFINITIVE
gesehen werden

3 FUTURE PASSIVE INDICATIVE
ich werde gesehen werden/wir werden gesehen werden *etc*

OR: **man wird mich/uns sehen** *etc*

4 FUTURE PASSIVE SUBJUNCTIVE
ich werde gesehen werden/wir werden gesehen werden *etc*

OR: **man werde mich/uns sehen** *etc*

5 PERFECT PASSIVE INFINITIVE
gesehen worden sein

6 FUTURE PERFECT PASSIVE
ich werde/wir werden gesehen worden sein *etc*

OR: **man wird mich/uns gesehen haben** *etc*

7 CONDITIONAL PASSIVE
ich würde gesehen werden/wir würden gesehen werden

OR: **man würde mich/uns sehen** *etc*

8 CONDITIONAL PERFECT PASSIVE
ich würde/wir würden gesehen worden sein

OR: **man würde mich/uns gesehen haben** *etc*
OR: pluperfect subjunctive: **man hätte mich/uns gesehen** *etc*

Impersonal Verbs

These verbs are used only in the third person singular, usually with the subject **es** meaning *it* (→1)

● Intransitive verbs (verbs with no direct object) are often made impersonal in the passive to describe activity of a general nature (→2)
  When the verb and subject are inverted (see p.226), the **es** is omitted (→3)
  Impersonal verbs in the passive can also be used as an imperative form (see p.20) (→4)

● In certain expressions in the active, the impersonal pronoun **es** can be omitted. In this case, a personal pronoun object begins the clause (→5)
  In the following lists * indicates that **es** may be omitted in this way:

Some common impersonal verbs and expressions

es donnert *it's thundering*
es fällt mir ein, daß/zu* *it occurs to me that/to* (→6)
es fragt sich, ob *one wonders whether* (→7)
es freut mich, daß/zu *I am glad that/to* (→8)
es friert *it is freezing* (→9)
es gefällt mir *I like it* (→10)
es geht mir gut/schlecht *I'm fine/not too good*
es geht nicht *it's not possible*
es geht um *it's about*
es gelingt mir, (zu) *I succeed (in)* (→11)
es geschieht *it happens* (→12)
es gießt *it's pouring*
es handelt sich um *it's a question of*
Continued

1 Es regnet It's raining

2 Es wurde viel gegessen und getrunken
There was a lot of eating and drinking

3 Auf der Hochzeit wurde viel gegessen und getrunken
There was a lot of eating and drinking at the wedding

4 Jetzt wird gearbeitet! Now you're going to work

5 Mir ist warm I'm warm

6 Nachher fiel (es) mir ein, daß der Mann ziemlich komisch angezogen war
Afterwards it occurred to me that the man was rather oddly dressed

7 Es fragt sich, ob es sich lohnt, das zu machen
One wonders if that's worth doing

8 Es freut mich sehr, daß du gekommen bist
I'm so pleased that you have come

9 Heute nacht hat es gefroren
It was below freezing last night

10 Ihm hat es gar nicht gefallen
He didn't like it at all

11 Es war ihnen gelungen, die letzten Karten zu kriegen
They had succeeded in getting the last tickets

12 Und so geschah es, daß ...
And so it came about that ...

Impersonal Verbs and Expressions (ctd.)

es hängt davon ab *it depends*
es hat keinen Zweck (zu) *there's no point (in)* (→1)
es interessiert mich, daß/zu* *I am interested that/to*
es ist mir egal (ob)* *it's all the same to me (if)* (→2)
es ist möglich (, daß) *it's possible (that)* (→3)
es ist nötig *it's necessary* (→4)
es ist mir, als ob* *I feel as if*
es ist mir gut/schlecht etc zumute* *I feel good /bad etc* (→5)
es ist schade (,daß) *it's a pity (that)*
es ist (mir) wichtig* *it's important (to me)*
es ist mir warm/kalt* *I'm hot/cold*
es ist warm/kalt *it's (the weather is) warm/cold*
es ist zu hoffen/bedauern etc* *it is to be hoped etc*
es klingelt *someone is ringing the bell* (→6)
es klopft *someone's knocking*
es kommt darauf an (, ob) *it all depends (whether)*
es kommt mir vor (, als ob) *it seems to me (as if)*
es läutet *the bell is ringing* (→7)
es liegt an *it is because of* (→8)
es lohnt sich (nicht) *it's (not) worth it* (→9)
es macht nichts *it doesn't matter*
es macht nichts aus *it makes no difference* (→10)
es macht mir (keinen) Spaß (, zu) *it's (no) fun (to)* (→11)
es passiert *it happens* (→12)
es regnet *it's raining* (→13)
es scheint mir, daß/als ob* *it seems to me that/as if*
es schneit *it's snowing*
es stellt sich heraus, daß *it turns out that*
es stimmt (nicht), daß *it's (not) true, that*
es tut mir leid (, daß) *I'm sorry (that)*
wie geht es (dir)? *how are you?* (→14)
mir wird schlecht* *I feel sick*

1 Es hat keinen Zweck, weiter darüber zu diskutieren
There's no point in discussing this any further

2 Es ist mir egal, ob du kommst oder nicht
I don't care if you come or not

3 Es ist doch möglich, daß der Zug Verspätung hat
It's always possible the train has been delayed

4 Es wird nicht nötig sein, uns darüber zu informieren
It won't be necessary to inform us of it

5 Mir ist heute seltsam zumute I feel strange today

6 Es hat gerade geklingelt
The bell just went/The phone just rang

7 Es hat schon geläutet The bell has gone

8 Woran liegt es? Why is that?

9 Ich weiß nicht, ob es sich lohnt oder nicht
I don't know if it's worth it or not

10 Mir macht es nichts aus It makes no difference to me
Macht es Ihnen etwas aus, wenn ... Would you mind if...

11 Hauptsache, es macht Spaß
The main thing is to enjoy yourself

12 Ihm ist bestimmt etwas passiert
Something must have happened to him

13 Es hat den ganzen Tag geregnet It rained the whole day

14 Wie geht's denn? — Danke, es geht
How are things? — Fine thank you

The Infinitive

Forms

There are four forms of the infinitive (→**1**). These forms are used in forming certain compound tenses (see p.28). The present active infinitive is the most widely used and is the form found in dictionaries.

Uses

● Preceded by **zu** (*to*)

1. as in English, after other verbs ("I tried *to come*") (→**2**)
2. as in English, after adjectives ("it was easy *to see*") (→**3**)
3. where the English equivalent is not always an infinitive:
   — after nouns, where English may use an "-ing" form (→**4**)
   — after **sein**, where the English equivalent may be a passive tense (→**5**)

● Without **zu**, the infinitive is used after the following:

    modal verbs (→**6**)
    lassen (→**7**)
    heißen (→**8**)
    bleiben (→**9**)
    gehen (→**10**)
    verbs of perception (→**11**)
    NOTE: verbs of perception can also be followed by a subordinate clause beginning with **wie** or **daß**, especially if the sentence is long or involved (→**12**)

Continued

1 INFINITIVES:

PRESENT ACTIVE	PERFECT ACTIVE
holen	**geholt haben**
to fetch	to have fetched
PRESENT PASSIVE	PERFECT PASSIVE
geholt werden	**geholt worden sein**
to be fetched	to have been fetched

2 Ich versuchte, zu kommen I tried to come

3 Es war leicht, zu sehen It was easy to see

4 Ich habe nur wenig Gelegenheit, Musik zu hören
I have little opportunity of listening to music

5 Er ist zu bedauern He is to be pitied

6 Er kann schwimmen He can swim

7 Sie ließen uns warten They kept us waiting

8 Er hieß ihn kommen He bade him come

9 Er blieb sitzen He remained seated

10 Sie ging einkaufen She went shopping

11 Ich sah ihn kommen I saw him coming
Er hörte sie singen He heard her singing

12 Er sah, wie sie langsam auf und ab schlenderte
He watched her strolling slowly up and down

The Infinitive (ctd.)

Used as an imperative
- The infinitive can be used as an imperative (see p.20) (→1)

Used as a noun
- The infinitive can be made into a noun by giving it a capital letter. Its gender is always neuter (→2)

Used with modal verbs (see p.52)
- An infinitive used with a modal verb is always placed at the end of a clause (see p.56) (→3)

- If the modal verb is in a compound tense, its auxiliary will follow the subject in a main clause in the normal way, and the modal participle comes after the infinitive. BUT in a subordinate clause, the auxiliary immediately precedes the infinitive and the modal participle, instead of coming at the end (→4)

- An infinitive expressing change of place may be omitted entirely after a modal verb (see p.56) (→5)

Used in infinitive phrases
Infinitive phrases can be formed with:

zu	ohne ... zu
um ... zu	anstatt ... zu (→6)

- The infinitive comes at the end of its phrase (→7)

- In separable verbs, **zu** is inserted *between* the verb and its prefix in the present infinitive (→8)

- A reflexive pronoun comes first, immediately following an introductory word if there is one (→9)

1 **Einsteigen und Türen schließen!**
All aboard! Close the doors!

2 **rauchen** to smoke:
Er hat das Rauchen aufgegeben
He's given up smoking

3 **Wir müssen morgen einkaufen gehen**
We have to go shopping tomorrow

4 **Sie haben gestern aufräumen müssen**
They had to tidy up yesterday
BUT
**Da sie gestern haben aufräumen müssen, durften sie nicht
kommen**
They couldn't come as they had to tidy up yesterday

5 **Er will jetzt nach Hause** He wants to go home now

6 **es zu tun** to do it
es getan zu haben to have done it
um es zu tun in order to do it
um es getan zu haben in order to have done it
ohne es zu tun without doing it
ohne es getan zu haben without having done it
anstatt es zu tun instead of doing it
anstatt es getan zu haben instead of having done it

7 **Ohne ein Wort zu sagen, verließ er das Haus**
He left the house without saying a word
Er ging nach Hause, ohne mit ihr gesprochen zu haben
He went home without having spoken to her

8 **aufgeben** to give up:
um es aufzugeben in order to give it up

9 **Sie gingen weg, ohne sich zu verabschieden**
They left without saying goodbye

The Present Participle

- The present participle for all verbs is formed by adding **-d** to the infinitive form (→**1**)

- The present participle may be used as an adjective. As with all adjectives, it is declined if used attributively (see p.140) (→**2**)

- The present participle may also be used as an adjectival noun (see p.148) (→**3**)

The Past Participle

- For weak verbs, the past participle is formed by prefixing **ge-** and adding **-t** to the verb stem (→**4**)

- For strong verbs, the past participle is formed by adding the prefix **ge-** and the ending **-en** to the verb stem (→**5**) The vowel is often modified too (→**6**) (See list of strong and mixed verbs beginning on p.86)

- Mixed verbs form their past participle by adding the **ge-** and **-t** of weak verbs, but they change their vowel as for strong verbs. (See list, p.86) (→**7**)

- The past participles of *separable* verbs are formed according to the above rules and are joined on to the separable prefix (→**8**)

- For *inseparable* verbs, past participles are formed without the **ge-** prefix (→**9**)

- Many past participles can also be used as adjectives and adjectival nouns (→**10**)

1 **lachen** to laugh
lachend laughing

singen to sing
singend singing

2 **ein lachendes Kind** a laughing child
mit klopfendem Herzen with beating heart

3 **der Vorsitzende/ein Vorsitzender** the/a chairman

4 **machen** to do/make
gemacht done/made

5 **sehen** to see
gesehen seen

6 **singen** to sing
gesungen sung

7 **wissen** to know
gewußt known

8 **aufstehen** to get up
aufgestanden got up

nachmachen to copy/imitate
nachgemacht imitated

9 **bestellen** to order
bestellt ordered

entscheiden to decide
entschieden decided

10 **seine verlorene Brille** his lost spectacles
Wir aßen Gebratenes We ate fried food

Modal Auxiliary Verbs

Modal verbs, sometimes called modal auxiliaries, are used to *modify* other verbs (to show e.g. possibility, ability, willingness, permission, necessity) much as in English:

> he *can* swim; *may* I come?; we *shouldn't* go

- In German the modal auxiliary verbs are: **dürfen, können, mögen, müssen, sollen** and **wollen**.

- Modal verbs have some important differences in their uses and in their conjugation from other verbs, and these are clearly shown on pp.86 to 97.

- Modal verbs have the following meanings:

dürfen   *to be allowed to/may* (→1)
used negatively: *must not/may not* (→2)
to show probability (→3)
also used in some polite expressions (→4)

können   *to be able to, can* (→5)
in its subjunctive forms:
would be able to/could (→6)
as an informal alternative to **dürfen** with the meaning: *allowed to/can* (→7)
to show possibility (→8)

mögen   *to like/to like to* (→9)
most common in its imperfect subjunctive form which expresses polite inquiry or request:
should like to/would like to (→10)
to show possibility or probability (→11)

Continued

Examples

1 Darfst du mit ins Kino kommen?
Are you allowed to (can you) come with us to the cinema?
Darf ich bitte mitkommen?
May I come with you please?
Ich dürfte schon, aber ich will nicht
I could (would be allowed to), but I don't want to
2 Hier darf man nicht rauchen
Smoking is prohibited here
3 Das dürfte wohl das Beste sein
That's probably the best thing
4 Was darf es sein?

5 Wir konnten es nicht schaffen
Can I help you?/What would you like?
6 Er könnte noch früher kommen
We couldn't (weren't able to) do it.
He could (would be able to) come even earlier
Er meinte, er könne noch früher kommen
He thought he could come earlier
Wir könnten vielleicht morgen hinfahren?
Perhaps we could go there tomorrow?
7 Kann ich (darf ich) ein Eis haben?
Can I (may I) have an ice-cream?
8 Wer könnte es gewesen sein?
Who could it have been?
Das kann sein
That may be so
BUT: **Das kann nicht sein.** That cannot be so
9 Magst du Butter?
Do you like butter?
10 Wir möchten bitte etwas trinken
We should like something to drink
Möchtest du sie besuchen?
Would you like to visit her?
11 Das Konzert möchte vier Stunden gedauert haben
The concert must have lasted four hours

Modal Auxiliary Verbs (ctd.)

müssen

to have to/must/need to (→1)
certain idiomatic uses (→2)

NOTE: for *must have ...* use the relevant tense
of **müssen** + past participle of main verb +
the auxiliary **haben** or **sein** (→3)
for *don't have to/need not*, a negative form of
brauchen (*to need*) may be used instead of
müssen (→4)

sollen

ought to/should (→5)
to be (supposed) to where the demand is not self-
imposed (→6)
to be said to be (→7)
as a command, either direct or indirect (→8)

wollen

to want/want to (→9)
used as a less formal version of **mögen** to
mean: *want/wish* (→10)
to be willing to (→11)
to show previous intention (→12)
to claim or pretend (→13)

Continued

Er hatte jeden Tag um sechs aufstehen müssen
He had to get up at six o'clock every day
Man mußte lachen
One had to laugh/couldn't help laughing

2 **Muß das sein?** Is that really necessary?
Ein Millionär müßte man sein!
Oh to be a millionaire!
Den Film muß man gesehen haben
That film is worth seeing

3 **Es muß geregnet haben** It must have been raining
Er meinte, es müsse am vorigen Abend passiert sein
He thought it must have happened the previous evening

4 **Das brauchtest du nicht zu sagen**
You didn't have to say that

5 **Man sollte immer die Wahrheit sagen**
One should always tell the truth
Er wußte nicht, was er tun sollte
He didn't know what to do (*what he should do*)

6 **Ich soll dir helfen**
I am to help you (*I have been told to help you*)
Du sollst sofort deine Frau anrufen
You are to 'phone your wife at once (*She has left a message asking you to ring*)

7 **Er soll sehr reich sein**
I've heard he's very rich/He is said to be very rich

8 **Es soll niemand sagen, daß die Schotten geizig sind!**
Let no-one say the Scots are mean!
Sie sagte mir, ich solle damit aufhören
She told me to stop it

9 **Das Kind will LKW-Fahrer werden**
The child wants to become a lorry driver

10 **Willst du eins?** Do you want one?
Willst du (möchtest du) etwas trinken?
Do you want (would you like) something to drink?

11 **Er wollte nichts sagen** He refused to say anything

12 **Ich wollte gerade anrufen** I was just about to 'phone

13 **Keiner will es gewesen sein** No-one admits to doing it

Modal Auxiliary Verbs (ctd.)

Conjugation and Use

- Modal verbs have unusual present tenses (→1)
  Their principal parts are given on pp.86 to 97.

- Each modal verb has two past participles.
  The first, which is the more common, is the same as the infinitive form and is used where the modal is modifying a verb (→2)
  The second resembles a normal weak past participle and is used only where no verb is being modified (see the verb list, p.86) (→3)

- The verb modified by the modal is placed in its infinitive form at the end of a clause (→4)

- Where the modal is used in a compound tense, its past participle in the form of the infinitive is also placed at the end of a clause, immediately after the modified verb (→5)

- If the modal verb is modifying a verb, and if the modal is used in a compound tense in a subordinate clause, then the normal word order for subordinate clauses (see p.228) does not apply. The auxiliary used to form the compound tense of the modal is not placed right at the end of the subordinate clause, but instead comes before both infinitives (→6)
  Such constructions are usually avoided in German, by using a simple tense in place of a compound. (For notes on the use of tenses in German, see p.58ff) (→7)

- A modified verb which expresses motion may be omitted entirely if an adverb or adverbial phrase is present to indicate the movement or destination (→8)

1 ich tue I do (*simple form*) OR I am doing (*continuous*)
 er rauchte he smoked OR he was smoking
 sie hat gelesen she has read OR she has been reading
 es ist geschickt worden it is sent OR it is being sent

2 Er kochte gerade das Abendessen
 He was cooking the supper
 Nun spricht sie mit ihm Now she's talking to him

3 Ich bin am Bügeln I am ironing

4 Wir waren eben dabei, einige Briefe zu schreiben
 We were just writing a few letters

5 Ich wohne seit zehn Jahren hier
 I have been living here for ten years
 Seit ich hier wohne, fühle ich mich wohl
 I've been feeling at home since I've lived here

6 Seit er krank ist, hat er uns nicht besucht
 He hasn't visited us since he's been ill
 Seit seiner Verlobung habe ich ihn nicht gesehen
 I haven't seen him since his engagement

7 Ich komme morgen vorbei I'll come round tomorrow
 Wir fahren nächstes Jahr nach Griechenland
 We're going to Greece next year

8 Das werde ich erst nächstes Jahr machen können
 I won't be able to do that until next year

9 Wenn er zurückkommt, wird er mir bestimmt helfen
 He's sure to help me when he returns

10 Ich werde ihm helfen I'm going to help him

11 Bis Sonntag wird er es gelesen haben
 He will have read it by Sunday

12 Es wird Herr Schmidt gewesen sein
 That must have been Herr Schmidt

13 Bis du zurückkommst, haben wir alles aufgeräumt
 We'll have tidied up by the time you get back

14 Wenn ich eins hätte, würde ich es dir geben
 If I had one I would give it to you
 Wenn er jetzt bloß kommen würde!
 If only he would get here!

15 Er fragte, ob wir fahren würden
 He asked if we were going to go

Use of Tenses (ctd.)

The Conditional Perfect
- May be used in place of the pluperfect subjunctive in a sentence containing a **wenn**-clause (→1)
- But the pluperfect subjunctive is preferred (→2)

The Imperfect
- Is used in German with **seit** or **seitdem** where the pluperfect is used in English to show an action which began in the remote past and continued to a point in the more recent past (→3)
  For discontinued actions the pluperfect is used (→4)
- Used to describe past actions which have no link with the present as far as the speaker is concerned (→5)
  for narrative purposes (→6)
  for repeated, habitual or prolonged past action (→7)
See also the note on the **Perfect** (below).

The Perfect
- Is used to translate the English perfect tense *I have spoken, he has been reading* (→8)
- Describes past actions or events which still have a link with the present or the speaker (→9)
- Is used in conversation and similar communication (→10)
NOTE: In practice however the perfect and imperfect are often interchangeable in German usage and in spoken German a mixture of both is common.

The Pluperfect
- Is used to translate *had done/had been doing*, except in conjunction with **seit/seitdem** (see Imperfect) (→11)

The Subjunctive
For uses of the subjunctive tenses, see pp.62 to 67.

1 Wenn du es gesehen hättest, würdest du's geglaubt haben
You would have believed it if you'd seen it

2 Hättest du es gesehen, so hättest du es geglaubt
If you had seen it, you'd have believed it
Wenn ich das nur nicht gemacht hätte!
If only I hadn't done it!
Wäre ich nur da gewesen! If I'd only been there

3 Sie war seit ihrer Heirat als Krankenschwester beschäftigt
She had been working as a nurse since her marriage

4 Ihren Sohn hatten sie seit zehn Jahren nicht gesehen
They hadn't seen their son for ten years

5 Er kam zu spät, um teilnehmen zu können
He arrived too late to take part

6 Das Mädchen stand auf, wusch sich das Gesicht, und verließ das Haus
The girl got up, washed her face and went out

7 Wir machten jeden Tag einen kleinen Spaziergang
We went (used to go) for a little walk every day

8 Ich habe ihn heute nicht gesehen
I haven't seen him today

9 Ich habe ihr nichts davon erzählt
I didn't tell her anything about it
Gestern sind wir in die Stadt gefahren, und haben uns ein Paar Sachen gekauft
Yesterday we went into town and bought ourselves a few things

10 Hast du den Krimi gestern abend im Fernsehen gesehen?
Did you see the thriller on television last night?

11 Sie waren schon weggefahren
They had already left
Diese Bücher hatten sie schon gelesen
They had already read these books

The Subjunctive: when to use it

The subjunctive form in English has almost died out, leaving only a few examples such as:
> if I *were* rich/if only he *were* to come/so *be* it

German however makes much wider use of subjunctive forms, especially in formal, educated or literary contexts. Although there is a growing tendency to use indicatives in spoken German, subjunctives are still very common.

- The indicative tenses in German display fact or certainty. The subjunctives show unreality, uncertainty, speculation about a situation or any doubt in the speaker's mind (→1) Subjunctives are also used in indirect speech, as shown on pp.66 and 67.

- For how to form all tenses of the subjunctive, the reader is referred to the relevant sections on Simple Tenses (pp.6 to 17) and Compound Tenses (pp.22 to 29). See also the Subjunctive in Reported Speech p.66.

- The **imperfect subjunctive** is very common. It is important to note that the imperfect subjunctive form does not always represent actions performed in the past (→2)

Uses of the Subjunctive in German

- To show improbable condition (e.g. if he *came*, he would ...)
  The *if*-clause (**wenn** in German) has a verb in the imperfect subjunctive and the main clause can have either an imperfect subjunctive or a conditional (→3)

Continued

1 INDICATIVE
Das stimmt
That's true
Es ist eine Unverschämtheit
It's a scandal

SUBJUNCTIVE
Es könnte doch wahr sein
It could well be true
Sie meint, es sei eine Unverschämtheit
She thinks it's a scandal (*speaker not necessarily in agreement with her*)

2 *imperfect subjunctive expressing the future*
Wenn ich morgen nur da sein könnte!
If only I could be there tomorrow!

expressing the present/immediate future
Wenn er jetzt nur käme!
If only he would come now!

speaker's opinion, referring to present or future
Sie wäre die Beste
She's the best

3 **Wenn du kämest, wäre ich froh**
OR
Wenn du kämest, würde ich froh sein
I should be happy if you came

Wenn es mir nicht gefiele, würde ich es nicht bezahlen
OR
Wenn es mir nicht gefiele, bezahlte ich es nicht
If I wasn't happy with it, I wouldn't pay for it
(*The second form is less likely, as the imperfect subjunctive and imperfect indicative forms of* **bezahlen** *are identical*)

The Subjunctive: when to use it (ctd.)

- The imperfect of **sollen** or **wollen**, or a conditional tense might be used in the **wenn**-clause to replace an uncommon imperfect subjunctive, or a subjunctive which is not distinct from the same tense of the indicative (→1)

- To show unfulfilled condition (if he *had come*, he would have...)
  The **wenn**-clause requires a pluperfect subjunctive, the main clause a pluperfect subjunctive or conditional perfect (→2)
  NOTE: The indicative is used to express a *probable* condition, as in English (→3)
  wenn can be omitted from conditional clauses. The verb must then follow the subject and **dann** or **so** usually begins the main clause (→4)

- With **selbst wenn** (*even if/even though*) (→5)

- With **wenn ... nur** (*if only ...*) (→6)

- To speculate or make assumptions (→7)

- After **als** (*as if/as though*) (→8)

- Where there is uncertainty or doubt (→9)

- To make a polite enquiry (→10)

- To indicate theoretical possibility or unreality (→11)

- As an alternative to the conditional perfect (→12)

1 Wenn er mich so sehen würde, würde er mich für verrückt halten!

OR

Wenn er mich so sehen sollte, hielte er mich für verrückt!

OR

Wenn er mich so sehen sollte, würde er mich für verrückt halten!

If he saw me like this, he would think I was mad!

(**Wenn er mich so sähe** *would sound rather stilted*)

2 Wenn du pünktlich gekommen wärest, hättest du ihn gesehen

OR

Wenn du pünktlich gekommen wärest, würdest du ihn gesehen haben

If you had been on time, you would have seen him

3 Wenn ich ihn sehe, gebe ich es ihm

If I see him I'll give him it

4 Hättest du mich nicht gesehen, so wäre ich schon weg

If you hadn't seen me, I would have been gone by now

5 Selbst wenn er etwas wüßte, würde er nichts sagen

Even if he knew about it, he wouldn't say anything

6 Wenn wir nur reich wären! If only we were rich!

7 Und wenn er recht hätte? What if he were right?

Eine Frau, die das sagen würde (*or* die das sagte), müßte Feministin sein!

Any woman who would say that must be a feminist!

8 Er sah aus, als sei er krank

He looked as if he were ill

9 Er wußte nicht, wie es ihr jetzt ginge

He didn't know how she was

10 Gäbe es sonst was? Will there be anything else?

11 Er dachte, wie er in dem Anzug gut aussähe

He thought how good he would look in the suit

12 Ich hätte ihn gesehen = Ich würde ihn gesehen haben

I would have seen him

The Subjunctive in Indirect Speech

What a person asks or thinks can be reported in one of two ways, either **directly**:

Tom said, "I have been on holiday"

OR **indirectly**:

Tom said (that) he had been on holiday

- In English, indirect, or reported, speech can be indicated by a change in tense of what has been reported:

    He said, *"I know your sister"*
    He said (that) *he knew* my sister

    In German the change is not in tense, but from indicative to subjunctive (→1)

- There are two ways of introducing indirect speech in German, similar to the parallel English constructions:
    1. The clause which reports what is said may be introduced by **daß** (*that*). The finite verb or auxiliary comes at the end of the clause (→2)
    2. **daß** may be omitted. The verb in this case must stand in second position in the clause, instead of being placed at the end (→3)

Forms of the Subjunctive in Indirect Speech

See the conjugation of verbs in the subjunctive pp.8 to 15 and 26 to 31. In indirect (or reported) speech, wherever the present subjunctive is identical to the present indicative form, the imperfect subjunctive is used instead (→4)

1 **Er sagte: "Sie kennt deine Schwester"**
He said, "She knows your sister"
Er sagte, sie kenne meine Schwester
He said she knew my sister
"Habe ich zu viel gesagt?", fragte er
"Did I say too much?", he asked
Er fragte, ob er zuviel gesagt habe
He asked if he had said too much

2 **Er hat uns gesagt, daß er Französisch spreche**
He told us that he spoke French

3 **Er hat uns gesagt, er spreche Französisch**
He told us he spoke French

4 PRESENT SUBJUNCTIVE IN INDIRECT SPEECH

WEAK VERBS e.g. **holen** to fetch :

ich holte	**wir holten**
du holest	ihr holet
er hole	**sie holten**

STRONG VERBS e.g. **singen** to sing :

ich sänge	**wir sängen**
du singest	ihr singet
er singe	**sie sängen**

Verbs with Prefixes

Many verbs in German begin with a prefix. A prefix is a word or part of a word which precedes the verb stem (→1)

- Often the addition of a prefix changes the meaning of the basic verb (→2)

- Prefixes may be found in strong, weak or mixed verbs. Adding a prefix may occasionally change the verb conjugation (→3)

- There are four kinds of prefix and each behaves in a slightly different way, as shown on the following pages. Prefixes may be:

> inseparable (→4)
>
> separable (→5)
>
> double (→6)
>
> variable, i.e. either separable or inseparable, depending on the verb (→7)

Continued

1 zu + geben   = **zugeben**
  an + ziehen = **anziehen**

2 **nehmen** to take
  zunehmen to put on weight, to increase
  sich benehmen to behave

3 WEAK: STRONG:
  suchen   to look for   **stehen**   to stand
  versuchen to try   **verstehen** to understand
  besuchen to visit   **aufstehen** to get up

  WEAK: WEAK:
  löschen   to extinguish   **fehlen**   to be missing
  STRONG: STRONG:
  erlöschen to go out   **empfehlen** to recommend

4 **entdecken** to discover
  er entdeckt, er entdeckte, er hat entdeckt

5 **mitmachen** to join in
  er macht mit, er machte mit, er hat mitgemacht

6 **ausverkaufen** to sell off
  er verkauft aus, er verkaufte aus, er hat ausverkauft

7 **wiederholen** to repeat
  er wiederholt, er wiederholte, er hat wiederholt

  wieder(-)holen to fetch back
  er holt wieder, er holte wieder, er hat wiedergeholt

Verbs with Prefixes (ctd.)

Inseparable Prefixes

- The eight inseparable prefixes are:

be-	emp-
ge-	ent-
er-	miß-
ver-	zer- (→1)

- These exist only as prefixes, and cannot be words in their own right.

- They are never separated from the verb stem, whatever tense of the verb is used (→2)

- Inseparable prefixes are always unstressed (→3)

- They have no **ge-** in their past participles (see p.50) (→4)

Continued

1 **beschreiben** to describe
  gehören to belong
  erhalten to contain
  verlieren to lose
  empfangen to receive
  enttäuschen to disappoint
  mißtrauen to mistrust
  zerlegen to dismantle

2 **besuchen** to visit:

  Er besucht uns regelmäßig
  He visits us regularly
  Er besuchte uns jeden Tag
  He used to visit us every day
  Er hat uns jeden Tag besucht
  He visited us every day
  Er wird uns morgen besuchen
  He will visit us tomorrow
  Besuche sofort deine Tante!
  Visit your aunt at once

3 erlauben,   verstehen,   empfangen,   vergessen

4 COMPARE:
  verstehen: wir haben verstanden we understood
  stehen: wir haben gestanden we stood

  empfangen: wir haben empfangen we received
  fangen: wir haben gefangen we caught

Verbs with Prefixes (ctd.)

Separable Prefixes

Some common examples are:

ab	empor	herbei	hinauf	nieder
an	entgegen	herein	hinaus	vor
auf	fest	herüber	hindurch	vorbei
aus	frei	herum	hinein	vorüber
bei	her	herunter	hinüber	weg
da(r)	herab	hervor	hinunter	zu
davon	heran	hierher	los	zurecht
dazu	herauf	hin	mit	zurück
ein	heraus	hinab	nach	zusammen

- Unlike inseparable prefixes, separable prefixes may be words in their own right. Indeed, nouns, adjectives, adverbs and even other verbs are often used as separable prefixes (→1)

- The past participle of a verb with a separable prefix is formed with **ge-**. It comes between the verb and the prefix (→2)

- In main clauses, the prefix is placed at the end of the clause if the verb is in a simple tense (i.e. present, imperfect or imperative form) (→3)

- In subordinate clauses, whatever the tense of the verb, the prefix is attached to the verb and the resulting whole placed at the end of the clause (→4)

- Where an infinitive construction requiring **zu** is used (see p.46), the **zu** is placed between the infinitive and prefix to form one word (→5)

1 *noun + verb*:   **teilnehmen** to take part
    verb + verb: **kennenlernen** to get to know
    adjective + verb: **loswerden** to get free of
    adverb + verb: **niederlegen** to lay down

2 Er ist gestern spazierengegangen
    He went for a walk yesterday
    Wir sind an der Grenze zurückgewiesen worden
    We were turned back at the border

3 **wegbringen**: to take for repair, to take away
    PRESENT : **Wir bringen das Auto weg**
    IMPERFECT : **Wir brachten das Auto weg**
    IMPERATIVE : **Bringt das Auto weg!**

    CONDITIONAL : **Wir würden das Auto wegbringen**
    FUTURE : **Wir werden das Auto wegbringen**
    PERFECT : **Wir haben das Auto weggebracht**
    PERFECT PASSIVE : **Das Auto ist weggebracht worden**
    PLUPERFECT SUBJUNCTIVE : **Wir hätten das Auto weggebracht**

4 PRESENT : **Weil wir das Auto wegbringen, ...**
    IMPERFECT : **Daß wir das Auto wegbrachten, ...**
    PERFECT : **Nachdem wir das Auto weggebracht haben, ...**
    PLUPERFECT SUBJUNCTIVE : **Wenn wir das Auto weggebracht
    hätten, ...**
    FUTURE : **Obwohl wir das Auto wegbringen werden, ...**

5 **Um das Auto rechtzeitig wegzubringen, müssen wir morgen
    früh aufstehen**
    In order to take the car in on time, we shall have to get up early

Verbs with Prefixes (ctd.)

Variable Prefixes

These are: über   um
            unter   voll
            durch   wider
            hinter   wieder

● These can be separable or inseparable (→1)

● Often they are used separably and inseparably with the same verb. In such cases the verb and prefix will tend to retain their basic meanings if the prefix is used separably, but adopt figurative meanings when the prefix is used inseparably (→2)

● Variable prefixes behave as separable prefixes when used separably, and as inseparable prefixes when used inseparably (→3)

Double Prefixes

These occur where a verb with an inseparable prefix is preceded by a separable prefix (→4)

● The separable prefix behaves as described on page 72, the verb plus inseparable prefix representing the basic verb to which the separable prefix is attached (→5)

● Unlike other separable verbs, however, verbs with double prefixes have no **ge-** in their past participles (→6)

1 unternehmen (*inseparable*) to undertake, take on:

Wir haben in den Ferien vieles unternommen
We did a great deal in the holidays
Du unternimmst zuviel
You take on too much

untergehen (*separable*) to sink, go down:

Die Sonne ist untergegangen
The sun has gone down/has set
Die Sonne geht unter
The sun is going down/is setting

2 etwas wiederholen (*separable*) to retrieve something
etwas wiederholen (*inseparable*) to repeat something

3 Er holte ihr die Tasche wieder
He brought her back her bag
Er wiederholte den Satz
He repeated the sentence

4 ausverkaufen to sell off

5 Er verkauft alles aus
He's selling everything off
Um alles auszuverkaufen ...
In order to sell everything off ...
Er wird alles ausverkaufen
He'll be selling everything off

6 Er hat doch alles ausverkauft
But he's sold everything off

Verbs followed by Prepositions

- Some verbs in English usage require a preposition (*for/with/by* etc) for their completion.
  This also happens in German, though the prepositions used with German verbs may not be those expected from their English counterparts (→**1**)

- The preposition used may significantly alter the meaning of a verb in German (→**2**)

- Occasionally German verbs use a preposition where their English equivalents do not (→**3**)

- Prepositions used with verbs behave as normal prepositions and affect the *case* of the following noun (see p.198).

- A verb plus preposition may be followed by a clause containing another verb rather than by a noun or pronoun. This often corresponds to an *-ing* construction in English:
  Thank you for *coming*
  In German, this is dealt with in two ways:
  1. Where the "verb-plus-preposition" construction has the same subject as the following verb, the preposition is preceded by **da-** or **dar-** and the following verb becomes an infinitive used with **zu** (→**4**)
  2. Where the subject of the "verb-plus-preposition" is not the same as for the following verb, a **daß** clause is used (→**5**)

- Following clauses may also be introduced by interrogatives (**ob**, **wie** etc) if the meaning demands them (→**6**)

Continued

1   Compare:

GERMAN	ENGLISH
sich sehnen **nach**	to long *for*
warten **auf**	to wait *for*
bitten **um**	to ask *for*

2   **bestehen** to pass (an examination/test *etc*)
    bestehen aus to consist of
    bestehen auf to insist on

    sich freuen auf to look forward to
    sich freuen über to be pleased about

3   **diskutieren über** to discuss

4   **Ich freue mich sehr darauf, mal wieder mit ihm zu arbeiten**
    I am looking forward to working with him again

5   **Ich freue mich sehr darauf, daß du morgen kommst**
    I am looking forward to your coming tomorrow
    Er sorgte dafür, daß die Kinder immer gut gepflegt waren
    He saw to it that the children were always well cared for

6   **Er dachte lange darüber nach, ob er es wirklich kaufen**
    wollte
    He thought for ages about whether he really wanted to buy it
    Sie freut sich darüber, wie ihre Schüler so schnell gelernt
    haben
    She is pleased at how quickly her students have learned

Verbs followed by Prepositions (ctd.)

Common verbs followed by preposition + accusative case:
achten auf to pay attention to, keep an eye on (→1)
sich amüsieren über to laugh at, smile about
sich ärgern über to get annoyed about/with
sich bewerben um to apply for (→2)
bitten um to ask for (→3)
denken an to be thinking of (→4)
denken über to hold an opinion of, think about (→5)
sich erinnern an to remember
sich freuen auf to look forward to
sich freuen über to be pleased about (→6)
sich gewöhnen an to get used to (→7)
sich interessieren für to be interested in (→8)
kämpfen um to fight for
sich kümmern um to take care of, see to
nachdenken über to ponder, reflect on (→9)
sich unterhalten über to talk about
sich verlassen auf to rely on, depend on (→10)
warten auf to wait for

Common verbs followed by preposition + dative case:
abhängen von to be dependent on (→11)
sich beschäftigen mit to occupy oneself with (→12)
bestehen aus to consist of (→13)
leiden an/unter to suffer from (→14)
neigen zu to be inclined to
riechen nach to smell of (→15)
schmecken nach to taste of
sich sehnen nach to long for
sterben an to die of
teilnehmen an to take part in (→16)
träumen von to dream of (→17)
sich verabschieden von to say goodbye to
sich verstehen mit to get along with, get on with
zittern vor to tremble with (→18)

1 Er mußte auf die Kinder achten
He had to keep an eye on the children

2 Sie hat sich um die Stelle als Buchhalterin beworben
She applied for the post of book-keeper

3 Die Kinder baten ihre Mutter um Plätzchen
The children asked their mother for some biscuits

4 Woran denkst du? What are you thinking about?
Daran habe ich gar nicht mehr gedacht
I'd forgotten about that

5 Wie denkt ihr darüber? What do you think about it?

6 Ich freute mich sehr darüber, Johann besucht zu haben
I was very glad I had visited Johann

7 Man gewöhnt sich an alles One gets used to anything

8 Sie interessiert sich sehr für Politik
She is very interested in politics

9 Er hatte schon lange darüber nachgedacht
He had been thinking about it for a long time

10 Er verläßt sich darauf, daß seine Frau alles tut
He relies on his wife to do everything

11 Das hängt davon ab It all depends

12 Sie sind im Moment sehr damit beschäftigt, ihr neues Haus in Ordnung zu bringen
They are very busy sorting out their new house at the moment

13 Dieser Kuchen besteht aus Eiern, Mehl und Zucker
This cake consists of eggs, flour and sugar

14 Sie hat lange an dieser Krankheit gelitten
She suffered from this illness for a long time
Alte Leute können sehr unter der Einsamkeit leiden
Old people can suffer dreadful loneliness

15 Der Kuchen hat nach Zimt gerochen
The cake smelled of cinnamon

16 Sie hat an der Bonner Tagung teilnehmen müssen
She had to attend the Bonn conference

17 Er hat von seinem Urlaub geträumt
He dreamt of his holiday

18 Er zitterte vor Freude He was trembling with joy

Verbs followed by the Dative

Some verbs have a direct object and an indirect object. In the English sentence *He gave me a book*, *me* (= *to me*) is the indirect object and would appear in the dative case in German; *a book* is the direct object of *gave* and would be in the accusative (→1)

- In German, as in English, this type of verb is usually concerned with giving or telling something to someone, or with performing an action for someone (→2)

- The normal word order after such verbs is for the direct object to follow the indirect, *except* where the direct object is a personal pronoun (see p.224) (→2)
  This order may be reversed for emphasis (→3)

- Some examples of verbs followed by the dative in this way:

anbieten	bringen	beweisen
erzählen	geben	gönnen
kaufen	leihen	mitteilen
schenken	schicken	schulden
schreiben	verkaufen	zeigen (→4)

- Certain verbs in German however can be followed *only* by an indirect object in the dative case. These should be noted especially, since most of them are quite different from their English equivalents:

begegnen	danken	fehlen
gefallen	gehören	gelingen
gleichen	gratulieren	helfen
imponieren	mißtrauen	nachgehen
schaden	schmecken	schmeicheln
trauen	trotzen	vorangehen
weh tun	widersprechen	widerstehen (→5)

- For how to form the passive of such verbs, see p.36.

1   **Er gab mir ein Buch** He gave me a book

2   **Er wusch dem Kind** (*indirect*) **das Gesicht** (*direct*)
He washed the child's face
Er erzählte ihm (*indirect*) **eine Geschichte** (*direct*)
He told him a story
BUT
Er hat sie (*direct*) **meiner Mutter** (*indirect*) **gezeigt**
He showed it to my mother
Kaufst du es (*direct*) **mir** (*indirect*)?
Will you buy it for me?

3   **Er wollte das Buch** (*dir.*) **seiner Mutter** (*indir.*) **geben**
(*This emphasises* **seiner Mutter**)
He wanted to give the book to his mother

4   **Er bot ihr den Zucker an** He offered her the sugar
Bringst du mir eins? Will you bring me one?
Ich gönne dir das neue Kleid
I want you to have the new dress
Er hat ihr mitgeteilt, daß ... He told her that ...
Ich schenke meiner Mutter Parfüm zum Geburtstag
I am giving my mother perfume for her birthday
Das schulde ich ihm I owe him that
Zeig es mir! Show me it!

6   **Er ist seinem Freund in der Stadt begegnet**
He bumped into his friend in town
Mir fehlt den Mut dazu I don't have the courage
Es ist ihnen gelungen They succeeded
Wem gehört dieses Buch? Whose book is this?
Er wollte ihr nicht helfen He refused to help her
Ich gratuliere dir! Congratulations!
Rauchen schadet der Gesundheit!
Smoking is bad for your health
Das Essen hat ihnen gut geschmeckt
They enjoyed the meal

There is/There are

There are three ways of expressing this in German:

es gibt

- This is always used in the singular form, and is followed by an accusative object which may be either singular or plural (→1)
- **es gibt** is used to refer to things of a general nature or location (→2)
- It also has some idiomatic usages (→3)

es ist/es sind

- The **es** here merely introduces the real subject. The verb therefore becomes plural where the real subject is plural. the real subject is in the nominative case (→4)
- The **es** is not required and is therefore omitted when the verb and real subject come together. This happens when inversion of subject and verb occurs (see p.226) and in subordinate clauses (→5)
- **es ist** or **es sind** are used to refer to
  1. subjects with a specific and confined location. This location must always be mentioned either by name or by **da, darauf, darin** etc (→6)
  2. temporary existence (→7)
  3. as a beginning to a story (→8)

The Passive Voice

Often *there is/there are* in English will be rendered by a verb in the passive voice in German (→9)

1 **Es gibt zu viele Probleme dabei**
   There are too many problems involved
   Es gibt kein Besseres bier
   There's no better beer

2 **Es gibt bestimmt Regen**
   It's definitely going to rain
   Ruhe hat es bei uns nie gegeben
   There has never been any peace here

3 **Was gibt's (= gibt es) zum Essen?** What's there to eat?
   Was gibt's? What's wrong? What's up?
   So was gibt's doch nicht! That's impossible!

4 **Es waren zwei ältere Leute unten im Hof**
   There were two elderly people down in the yard
   Es sind so viele Touristen da
   There are so many tourists there

5 **Unten im Hof waren zwei ältere Leute**
   Down in the yard were two elderly people
   Wenn so viele Touristen da sind ...
   If there are so many tourists there ...

6 **Es waren viele Flaschen Sekt im Keller**
   There were a lot of bottles of champagne in the cellar
   **Ein Brief lag auf dem Tisch. Es waren auch zwei Bücher
   darauf**
   A letter lay on the table. There were also two books on it

7 **Es war niemand da** There was no-one there

8 **Es war einmal ein König ...**
   Once upon a time there was a king ...

9 **Es wurde auf der Party viel getrunken**
   There was a lot of drinking at the party

Use of "es" as an anticipatory object

Many verbs can have as their object a **daß** clause or an infinitive with **zu** (→1)

● With some verbs **es** is used as an object to anticipate this clause or infinitive phrase (→2)
● When the clause or infinitive phrase begins the sentence, **es** is not used in the main clause but its place may be taken by an optional **das** (→3)

Common verbs which usually have the "es" object

es ablehnen, zu to refuse to
es aushalten, zu tun/daß to stand doing (→4)
es ertragen, zu tun/daß to endure doing
es leicht haben, zu to find it easy to (→5)
es nötig haben, zu to need to (→6)
es satt haben, zu to have had enough of (doing)
es verstehen, zu to know how to (→7)

Common verbs which often have the "es" object

es jemandem anhören/ansehen, daß to tell by listening to/looking at somone that (→8)
es begreifen, daß/warum/wie to understand that/why/how
es bereuen, zu tun/daß to regret having done/that
es leugnen, daß to deny that (→9)
es unternehmen, zu to undertake to
es jemandem verbieten, zu to forbid someone to
es jemandem vergeben, daß to forgive someone for (doing)
es jemandem verschweigen, daß not to tell someone that
es jemandem verzeihen, daß to forgive someone for (doing)
es wagen zu to dare to

1 **Er wußte, daß wir pünktlich kommen würden**
He knew that we would come on time
Sie fing an zu lachen
She began to laugh

2 **Er hatte es abgelehnt mitzufahren**
He had refused to come

3 **Daß es Peter war, das haben wir ihr verschwiegen**
OR: **Daß es Peter war, haben wir ihr verschwiegen**
We didn't tell her that it was Peter

4 **Ich halte es nicht mehr aus, bei ihnen zu arbeiten**
I can't stand working for them any longer

5 **Er hatte es nicht leicht, sie zu überreden**
He didn't have an easy job persuading them

6 **Ich habe es nicht nötig, mit dir darüber zu reden**
I don't have to talk to you about it

7 **Er versteht es, Autos zu reparieren**
He knows about repairing cars

8 **Man hörte es ihm sofort an, daß er kein Deutscher war**
OR: **Daß er kein Deutscher war, (das) hörte man ihm sofort an**
One could tell immediately (from the way he spoke) that he wasn't German

    Man sieht es ihm sofort an, daß er dein Bruder ist
OR: **Daß er dein Bruder ist, (das) sieht man ihm sofort an**
One can tell at a glance that he's your brother

9 **Er hat es nie geleugnet, das Geld genommen zu haben**
He has never denied taking the money

Strong and Mixed Verbs - Principal Parts

INFINITIVE

3RD PERSON
PRESENT

backen	to bake	er **bäckt**
befehlen	to command	er **befiehlt**
beginnen	to begin	er **beginnt**
beißen	to bite	er **beißt**
bergen	to rescue	er **birgt**
bersten	to burst *intr*	er **birst**
betrügen	to deceive	er **betrügt**
biegen	to bend *tr*/to turn *intr*	er **biegt**
bieten	to offer	er **bietet**
binden	to tie	er **bindet**
bitten	to ask for	er **bittet**
blasen	to blow	er **bläst**
bleiben	to remain	er **bleibt**
braten	to fry	er **brät**
brechen	to break	er **bricht**
brennen	to burn	er **brennt**
bringen	to bring	er **bringt**
denken	to think	er **denkt**
dreschen	to thresh	er **drischt**
dringen	to penetrate	er **dringt**
dürfen	to be allowed to	er **darf**
empfehlen	to recommend	er **empfiehlt**
erlöschen	to go out (*fire, light*)	er **erlischt**
erschallen	to resound	er **erschallt**
erschrecken	to be startled[1]	er **erschrickt**
erwägen	to weigh up	er **erwägt**
essen	to eat	er **ißt**
fahren	to travel	er **fährt**

1. **erschrecken** meaning "to frighten" is **weak**:
   erschrecken, erschreckt, erschreckte, hat
   erschreckt

3RD PERSON IMPERFECT	PERFECT	IMPERFECT SUBJUNCTIVE
er backte	er hat gebacken	er backte
er befahl	er hat befohlen	er befähle
er begann	er hat begonnen	er begänne
er biß	er hat gebissen	er bisse
er barg	er hat geborgen	er bärge
er barst	er ist geborsten	er bärste
er betrog	er hat betrogen	er betröge
er bog	er hat/ist gebogen	er böge
er bot	er hat geboten	er böte
er band	er hat gebunden	er bände
er bat	er hat gebeten	er bäte
er blies	er hat geblasen	er bliese
er blieb	er ist geblieben	er bliebe
er briet	er hat gebraten	er briete
er brach	er hat/ist gebrochen	er bräche
er brannte	er hat gebrannt	er brennte
er brachte	er hat gebracht	er brächte
er dachte	er hat gedacht	er dächte
er drosch	er hat gedroschen	er drösche
er drang	er ist gedrungen	er dränge
er durfte	er hat gedurft/dürfen[1]	er dürfte
er empfahl	er hat empfohlen	er empfähle
er erlosch	er ist erloschen	er erlösche
er erschallte	er ist erschollen	er erschölle
er erschrak	er ist erschrocken	er erschräke
er erwog	er hat erwogen	er erwöge
er aß	er hat gegessen	er äße
er fuhr	er ist gefahren	er führe

1. The second (infinitive) form is used when combined with an infinitive construction (see p.56).

Continued

INFINITIVE		3RD PERSON PRESENT
fallen	to fall	er **fällt**
fangen	to catch	er **fängt**
fechten	to fight	er **ficht**
finden	to find	er **findet**
fliegen	to fly	er **fliegt**
fliehen	to flee *tr/intr*	er **flieht**
fließen	to flow	er **fließt**
fressen	to eat (*of animals*)	er **frißt**
frieren	to be cold; freeze over	er **friert**
gebären	to give birth to	sie **gebärt**
geben	to give	er **gibt**
gedeihen	to thrive	er **gedeiht**
gehen	to go	er **geht**
gelingen	to succeed	es **gelingt**
gelten	to be valid	er **gilt**
genesen	to get well	er **genest**
genießen	to enjoy	er **genießt**
geraten	to get into (*a state etc*)	er **gerät**
geschehen	to happen	er **geschieht**
gewinnen	to win	er **gewinnt**
gießen	to pour	er **gießt**
gleichen	to resemble; equal	er **gleicht**
gleiten	to glide	er **gleitet**
glimmen	to glimmer	er **glimmt**
graben	to dig	er **gräbt**
greifen	to grip	er **greift**
haben	to have	er **hat**
halten	to hold, stop	er **hält**
hängen	to hang *intr*[1]	er **hängt**
heben	to lift	er **hebt**
heißen	to be called	er **heißt**

1. **hängen** is **weak** when used transitively.

3RD PERSON IMPERFECT	PERFECT	IMPERFECT SUBJUNCTIVE
er fiel	er ist gefallen	er fiele
er fing	er hat gefangen	er finge
er focht	er hat gefochten	er föchte
er fand	er hat gefunden	er fände
er flog	er hat/ist geflogen	er flöge
er floh	er hat/ist geflohen	er flöhe
er floß	er ist geflossen	er flösse
er fraß	er hat gefressen	er fräße
er fror	er hat/ist gefroren	er fröre
sie gebar	sie hat geboren	sie gebäre
er gab	er hat gegeben	er gäbe
er gedieh	er ist gediehen	er gediehe
er ging	er ist gegangen	er ginge
es gelang	es ist gelungen	es gelänge
er galt	er hat gegolten	er gälte
er genas	er ist genesen	er genäse
er genoß	er hat genossen	er genösse
er geriet	er ist geraten	er geriete
er geschah	er ist geschehen	er geschähe
er gewann	er ist gewonnen	er gewönne
er goß	er hat gegossen	er gösse
er glich	er hat geglichen	er gliche
er glitt	er ist geglitten	er glitte
er glomm	er hat geglommen	er glömme
er grub	er hat gegraben	er grübe
er griff	er hat gegriffen	er griffe
er hatte	er hat gehabt	er hätte
er hielt	er hat gehalten	er hielte
er hing	er hat gehangen	er hinge
er hob	er hat gehoben	er höbe
er hieß	er hat geheißen	er hieße

Continued

INFINITIVE		3RD PERSON PRESENT
helfen	to help	**er hilft**
kennen	to know (*someone etc*)	**er kennt**
klingen	to sound	**er klingt**
kommen	to come	**er kommt**
kneifen	to pinch	**er kneift**
können	to be able to	**er kann**
kriechen	to crawl	**er kriecht**
laden	to load	**er lädt**
lassen	to allow	**er läßt**
laufen	to walk; run	**er läuft**
leiden	to suffer	**er leidet**
leihen	to lend	**er leiht**
lesen	to read	**er liest**
liegen	to lie	**er liegt**
lügen	to tell a lie	**er lügt**
mahlen	to grind	**er mahlt**
messen	to measure	**er mißt**
mißlingen	to fail	**es mißlingt**
mögen	to like to	**er mag**
müssen	to have to	**er muß**
nehmen	to take	**er nimmt**
nennen	to call	**er nennt**
pfeifen	to whistle	**er pfeift**
preisen	to praise	**er preist**
quellen	to gush	**er quillt**
raten	to advise; guess	**er rät**
reiben	to rub	**er reibt**
reißen	to tear *tr/intr*	**er reißt**
reiten	to ride *tr/intr*	**er reitet**

3RD PERSON IMPERFECT	PERFECT	IMPERFECT SUBJUNCTIVE
er half	er hat geholfen	er hülfe
er kannte	er hat gekannt	er kennte
er klang	er hat geklungen	er klänge
er kam	er ist gekommen	er käme
er kniff	er hat gekniffen	er kniffe
er konnte	er hat gekonnt/können[1]	er könnte
er kroch	er ist gekrochen	er kröche
er lud	er hat geladen	er lüde
er ließ	er hat gelassen	er ließe
er lief	er ist gelaufen	er liefe
er litt	er hat gelitten	er litte
er lieh	er hat geliehen	er liehe
er las	er hat gelesen	er läse
er lag	er hat gelegen	er läge
er log	er hat gelogen	er löge
er mahlte	er hat gemahlen	er mahlte
er maß	er hat gemessen	er mäße
es mißlang	es ist mißlungen	es mißlänge
er mochte	er hat gemocht/mögen[1]	er möchte
er mußte	er hat gemußt/müssen[1]	er müßte
er nahm	er hat genommen	er nähme
er nannte	er hat genannt	er nennte
er pfiff	er hat gepfiffen	er pfiffe
er pries	er hat gepriesen	er priese
er quoll	er ist gequollen	er quölle
er riet	er hat geraten	er riete
er rieb	er hat gerieben	er riebe
er riß	er hat/ist gerissen	er risse
er ritt	er hat/ist geritten	er ritte

1. The second (infinitive) form is used when combined with an infinitive construction (see p.56).

Continued

INFINITIVE		3RD PERSON PRESENT
rennen	to run	er rennt
riechen	to smell	er riecht
ringen	to wrestle	er ringt
rinnen	to flow	er rinnt
rufen	to shout	er ruft
salzen	to salt	er salzt
saufen	to booze; drink	er säuft
saugen	to suck	er saugt
schaffen	to create[1]	er schafft
scheiden	to separate *tr/intr*	er scheidet
scheinen	to seem; shine	er scheint
schelten	to scold	er schilt
scheren	to shear	er schert
schieben	to shove	er schiebt
schießen	to shoot	er schießt
schlafen	to sleep	er schläft
schlagen	to hit	er schlägt
schleichen	to creep	er schleicht
schleifen	to grind	er schleift
schließen	to close	er schließt
schlingen	to wind	er schlingt
schmeißen	to fling	er schmeißt
schmelzen	to melt *tr/intr*	er schmilzt
schneiden	to cut	er schneidet
schreiben	to write	er schreibt
schreien	to shout	er schreit
schreiten	to stride	er schreitet
schweigen	to be silent	er schweigt

1. **schaffen** meaning "to work hard/manage" is **weak**:
   schaffen, schafft, schaffte, hat geschafft

3RD PERSON IMPERFECT	PERFECT	IMPERFECT SUBJUNCTIVE
er trug	er hat getragen	er trüge
er traf	er hat getroffen	er träfe
er trieb	er hat getrieben	er triebe
er trat	er hat/ist getreten	er träte
er trank	er hat getrunken	er tränke
er tat	er hat getan	er täte
er verdarb	er hat/ist verdorben	er verdürbe
er verdroß	er hat verdrossen	er verdrösse
er vergaß	er hat vergessen	er vergäße
er verlor	er hat verloren	er verlöre
er vermied	er hat vermieden	er vermiede
er verschwand	er ist verschwunden	er verschwände
er verzieh	er hat verziehen	er verziehe
er wuchs	er ist gewachsen	er wüchse
er wusch	er hat gewaschen	er wüsche
er wich	er ist gewichen	er wiche
er wies	er hat gewiesen	er wiese
er wandte	er hat gewandt	er wendete
er warb	er hat geworben	er würbe
er wurde	er ist geworden	er würde
er warf	er hat geworfen	er würfe
er wog	er hat gewogen	er wöge
er wand	er hat gewunden	er wände
er wußte	er hat gewußt	er wüßte
er wollte	er hat gewollt/wollen[1]	er wollte
er zog	er hat gezogen	er zöge
er zwang	er hat gezwungen	er zwänge

1. The second (infinitive) form is used when combined with an infinitive construction (see p.56).

The Declension of Nouns

In German, all nouns may be declined. This means that they may change their form according to their

>   *gender* (i.e. masculine, feminine or neuter) (→1)
>
>   *case* (i.e. their function in the sentence) (→2)
>
>   *number* (i.e. singular or plural) (→3)

- Nearly all *feminine* nouns change in the *plural* form by adding **-n** or **-en**. Many *masculine* and *neuter* nouns also change (→4)

- *Masculine* and *neuter* nouns, with a few exceptions, add **-s** (**-s** or **-es** for nouns of one syllable) in the *genitive singular* (but see p.110) (→5)

- All nouns end in **-n** or **-en** in the *dative plural*. This is added to the nominative plural form, where this does not already end in **-n** (→6)

- A good dictionary will provide guidance in how to decline a noun:
  The nominative singular form is given in full, followed by the gender of the noun, then the genitive singular and nominative plural endings are shown where appropriate (→7)

- Adjectives used as nouns are declined as adjectives rather than nouns. Their declension endings are therefore dictated by the preceding article, as well as by number, case and gender (see p.140) (→8)

Continued

1 der Tisch (*masculine*) the table
  die Gabel (*feminine*) the fork
  das Mädchen (*neuter*) the girl

2 des Tisches of the table
  auf den Tischen on the tables

3 die Tische the tables
  die Gabeln the forks
  die Mädchen the girls

4

	NOM. SING.	NOM. PLURAL
MASC	der Apfel	die Äpfel
FEM	die Schule	die Schulen
NEUT	das Kind	die Kinder

5

	NOM. SING.	GEN. SING.
MASC	der Apfel	des Apfels
FEM	die Schule	der Schule
NEUT	das Kind	des Kind(e)s

6 den Äpfeln
  den Schulen
  den Kindern

7 Tiger *m* —s, —

NOM. SING.	der Tiger	the tiger
GEN. SING.	des Tigers	of the tiger, the tiger's
NOM. PL.	die Tiger	the tigers

8 der Angestellte the employee
  ein Angestellter an employee
  (die) Angestellten (the) employees

The Gender of Nouns

In German a noun may be masculine, feminine or neuter.
Gender is relatively unpredictable and has to be learned for
each noun. This is best done by learning each noun with its
definite article, i.e.

der Teppich, die Zeit, das Bild

The following are intended therefore only as guidelines in
helping decide the gender of a word.

- Nouns denoting male people and animals are masculine
  (→**1**)

- Nouns denoting the female of the species, as shown on
  p.104 are of course feminine (→**2**)

- But nouns denoting an entire species can be of any gender
  (→**3**)

- Makes of cars identify with **der Wagen** and so are usually
  masculine (→**4**)

- Makes of aeroplane usually identify with **die Maschine**
  and so are feminine (→**5**)

- Seasons, months, days of the week, weather features and
  north, south, east, west are masculine (→**6**)

- Names of objects that perform an action are usually
  masculine (→**7**)

- Foreign nouns ending in **-ant, -ast, -ismus, -or** are
  masculine (→**8**) (But see the list of exceptions below)

- Nouns ending in **-ich, -ig, -ing, -ling** are masculine (→**9**)

Continued

1 der **Hörer** (male) listener
der **Löwe** (male) lion
der **Onkel** uncle
der **Vetter** (male) cousin

2 die **Hörerin** (female) listener
die **Löwin** lioness
die **Tante** aunt
die **Kusine** (female) cousin

3 der **Hund** dog
die **Schlange** snake
das **Vieh** cattle

4 der **Mercedes** Mercedes
der **VW** Volkswagen

5 die **Boeing** Boeing
die **Concorde** Concorde

6 der **Sommer** summer
der **Winter** winter
der **August** August
der **Freitag** Friday
der **Wind** wind
der **Schnee** snow
der **Norden** north
der **Osten** east

7 der **Wecker** alarm clock
der **Computer** computer

8 der **Ballast** ballast
der **Chauvinismus** chauvinism

9 der **Essig** vinegar
der **Schmetterling** butterfly

The Gender of Nouns (ctd.)

- Cardinal numbers are mostly feminine, but fractions are neuter (→1)

- Most nouns ending in **-e** are feminine (→2)
  EXCEPTIONS: male people or animals are masculine (→3)
                 nouns beginning with **Ge-** are normally neuter (→4)

- Nouns ending in **-heit, -keit, -schaft, -ung, -ei** are feminine (→5)

- Foreign nouns ending in **-anz, -enz, -ie, -ik, -ion, -tät, -ur** are generally feminine (→6)

- Nouns denoting the young of a species are neuter (→7)

- Infinitives used as nouns are neuter (→8)

- Most nouns beginning with **Ge-** are neuter (→9)

- **-chen** or **-lein** may be added to many words to give a diminutive form. These words are then neuter (→10)
  Note that the vowel adds an umlaut where possible (i.e. on **a, o, u** or **au**) and a final **-e** is dropped before these endings (→11)

- Nouns ending in **-nis** or **-tum** are neuter (→12)

- Foreign nouns ending in **-at, -ett, -fon, -ma, -ment, -um, -ium** are mainly neuter (→13)

- Adjectives and participles may be used as masculine, feminine or neuter nouns (see p.148) (→14)

Continued

1 Er hat eine Drei gekriegt He got a three (*mark*)
  ein Drittel davon a third of it
2 die Falte crease, wrinkle
  die Brücke bridge
3 der Löwe lion
  der Matrose sailor
4 das Getreide crops
  das Gelände terrain, grounds
5 die Eitelkeit vanity
  die Gewerkschaft trade union
  die Scheidung divorce
  die Druckerei printing works
6 die Distanz distance
  die Konkurrenz rivalry
  die Theorie theory
  die Panik panic
  die Union union
  die Elektrizität electricity
  die Partitur score (*musical*)
7 das Baby baby
  das Kind child
8 das Schwimmen swimming
9 das Geschirr crockery, dishes
  das Geschöpf creature
10 das Kindlein child
11 das Fräulein young lady (*from* **die Frau**)
  das Kätzchen kitten (*from* **die Katze**)
12 das Ereignis event
  das Altertum antiquity
13 das Tablett tray
  das Telefon telephone
  das Testament will
  das Podium platform, podium
14 der Verwandte male relative
  die Verwandte female relative
  die Neuen new things

The Gender of Nouns

The following are some common exceptions to the gender guidelines shown on pp.100 to 103

> **das Weib** woman, wife
> **die Person** person
> **die Waise** orphan
> **das Mitglied** member
> **das Genie** genius
> **die Wache** sentry, guard
> **das Restaurant** restaurant

The Formation of Feminine Nouns

As in English, male and female forms are sometimes shown by two completely different words, e.g.

> *mother/father, uncle/aunt etc* (→1)

Where such separate forms do not exist, however, German often differentiates between male and female forms in one of two ways:

- The masculine form may sometimes be made feminine by the addition of **-in** in the singular and **-innen** in the plural (→2)

- An adjective may be used as a feminine noun (see p.148). It has feminine adjective endings which change according to the article which precedes it (see p.140) (→3)

Continued

1 **der Vater**   **die Mutter**
      father   mother
      der Bulle   **die Kuh**
      bull   cow
      der Mann   **die Frau**
      man   woman

2 **der Lehrer**   **die Lehrerin**
      (male) teacher   (female) teacher
      der König   **die Königin**
      king   queen
      der Hörer   **die Hörerin**
      (male) listener   (female) listener

HENCE:
Liebe Hörer und Hörerinnen! Dear listeners!
unsere Leser und Leserinnen our readers

3 **eine Deutsche** a German woman
      Er ist mit einer Deutschen verheiratet
      He is married to a German
      die Abgeordnete the female MP
      Nur Abgeordnete durften dabeisein
      Only MP's were allowed in

The Gender of Nouns: miscellaneous points

Compound Nouns

Compound nouns, i.e. nouns composed of two or more nouns put together, are a regular feature of German.

- They normally take their gender and declension from the last noun of the compound word (→**1**)

- Exceptions to this are compounds ending in **-mut**, **-scheu** and **-wort**, which do not always have the same gender as the last word when it stands alone (→**2**)

Nouns with more than one gender

- A few nouns have two genders, either of which is acceptable (→**3**)

- Other nouns have two genders, each of which gives the noun a different meaning. (→**4**)

Abbreviations

- These take the gender of their principal noun (→**5**)

1 die **Armbanduhr** wristwatch (*from* die Uhr)
der **Tomatensalat** tomato salad (*from* der Salat)
der **Schlagzeugspieler** percussionist (*from* der Spieler)

2 der **Mut** courage
die **Armut** poverty
die **Demut** humility

die **Scheu** fear, shyness, timidity
der **Abscheu** repugnance, abhorrence

das **Wort** word
die **Antwort** reply

3 das/der **Radio** radio
das/der **Keks** biscuit

4 der **Band** volume, book
das **Band** ribbon, band, tape, bond
der **See** lake
die **See** sea
der **Leiter** leader, manager
die **Leiter** ladder
der **Tau** dew
das **Tau** rope, hawser

5 die **DDR** the German Democratic Republic (*from* die Deutsche Demokratische Republik)
die **BRD** the Federal Republic of Germany (*from* die Bundesrepublik Deutschland)
die **EG** the EEC (*from* die Europäische Gemeinschaft)

The Cases

There are four grammatical *cases*, which are generally shown by the form of the article used before the noun (see p.118).

The nominative case

- The nominative singular is the form shown in full in dictionary entries. The nominative plural is formed as described on p.98.

- The nominative case is used for:
  — the subject of a verb (→**1**)
  — the complement of **sein** or **werden** (→**2**)

The accusative case

- The noun in the accusative case usually has the same form as in the nominative (→**3**)
  Exceptions to this are "weak" masculine nouns (see p.115) and adjectives used as nouns (see p.148).

- It is used:
  — for the direct object of the verb (→**4**)
  — after those prepositions which always take the accusative case (see p.206ff) (→**5**)
  — to show change of location after prepositions of place (see p. 210) (→**6**)
  — in many expressions of time and place which do not contain a preposition (→**7**)
  — in certain fixed expressions (→**8**)

Continued

1 Das Mädchen singt The girl is singing

2 Er ist ein guter Lehrer He's a good teacher
   Das wird ein Pullover It's going to be a jumper

3 das Lied the song (*nominative*)
   das Lied the song (*accusative*)
   der Wagen the car (*nominative*)
   den Wagen the car (*accusative*)
   die Dose the tin (*nominative*)
   die Dose the tin (*accusative*)

4 Er hat ein Lied gesungen He sang a song

5 für seine Freundin for his girlfriend
   ohne diesen Wagen without this car
   durch das Rauchen through smoking

6 in die Stadt (*accusative*) into town
   BUT:
   in der Stadt (*dative*) in town

7 Das macht sie jeden Donnerstag
   She does that every Thursday
   Die Schule ist eine Kilometer entfernt
   The school is a kilometer away

8 Guten Abend! Good evening!
   Vielen Dank! Thank you very much!

The Cases (ctd.)

The genitive case

- In the genitive singular, *masculine* and *neuter* nouns take endings as follows:
  1) **-s** is added to nouns ending in **-en, -el, -er** (→1)
  2) **-es** is added to nouns ending in **-tz, -sch, -st** or **-ß** (→2)
  3) For nouns of one syllable, either **-s** or **-es** may be added (→3)
- *Feminine singular* and all *plural* nouns have the same form as their nominative.
- The genitive is used:
  — to show possession   (→3)
  — after prepositions taking the genitive (see p.212) (→4)
  — in expressions of time when the exact occasion is not specified (→5)

The dative case

- Singular nouns in the dative have the same form as in the nominative (→6)
- **-e** may be added to the dative singular of *masculine* and *neuter* nouns if the sentence rhythm needs it (→7)
  This **-e** is always used in certain set phrases (→8)
- Dative plural forms for all genders end in **-n** (→9)
  The only exceptions to this are some nouns of foreign origin that end in **-s** in all plural forms, including the dative plural (see p.114) (→10)
- The dative is used:
  — as the indirect object   (→11)
  — after verbs taking the dative (see p.80) (→12)
  — after prepositions taking the dative (see p.202) (→13)
  — in certain idiomatic expressions (→14)
  — instead of the possessive adjective to refer to parts of the body and items of clothing (see p.122) (→15)

1 der Wagen car → **des Wagens** of the car
  das Rauchen smoking → **des Rauchens** of smoking
  der Computer computer → **des Computers** of the computer
  der Reiter rider → **des Reiters** of the rider

2 der Sitz seat; residence → **des Sitzes** of the seat/residence
  der Arzt doctor → **des Arztes** of the doctor
  das Schloß castle → **des Schlosses** of the castle

3 das Kind →
  Die Zähne des Kindes waren faul geworden
  The child's teeth had decayed
  Der Name des Kinds war ihm unbekannt
  The child's name was not known to him

4 wegen seiner Krankheit because of his illness
  trotz ihrer Bemühungen despite her efforts

5 eines Tages one day

6 dem Wagen to the car
  der Frau to the woman
  dem Mädchen to the girl

7 zu welchem Zwecke? to what purpose?

8 nach Hause home
  sich zu Tode trinken/arbeiten
  to drink/work oneself to death

9 mit den Anwälten with the lawyers
  nach den Kindern after the children

10

SINGULAR	PLURAL
das Auto	die Autos
das Auto	die Autos
des Autos	der Autos
dem Auto	den Autos

11 Er gab dem Mann das Buch He gave the man the book
12 Sie half ihrer Mutter She helped her mother
13 Nach dem Essen ... After eating ...
14 Mir ist kalt I'm cold
15 Ich habe mir die Hände gewaschen I've washed my hands

The Formation of Plurals

The following pages show full noun declensions in all their singular and plural forms.

Those nouns shown represent the most common types of plural.

- Most feminine nouns add **-n**, **-en** or **-nen** to form their plurals:

	singular	plural
nom	**die Frau**	**die Frauen**
acc	**die Frau**	**die Frauen**
gen	**der Frau**	**der Frauen**
dat	**der Frau**	**den Frauen**

- Many nouns have no plural ending.
  These are mainly masculine or neuter nouns ending in **-en**, **-er**, **-el**.
  An umlaut is sometimes added to the vowel in the plural forms.

	singular	plural
nom	**der Onkel**	**die Onkel**
acc	**den Onkel**	**die Onkel**
gen	**des Onkels**	**der Onkel**
dat	**dem Onkel**	**den Onkeln**

	singular	plural
nom	**der Apfel**	**die Äpfel**
acc	**den Apfel**	**die Äpfel**
gen	**des Apfels**	**der Äpfel**
dat	**dem Apfel**	**den Äpfeln**

Continued

The Formation of Plurals (ctd.)

● Many nouns form their plurals by adding ⸚e

	singular	plural
nom	**der Stuhl**	**die Stühle**
acc	**den Stuhl**	**die Stühle**
gen	**des Stuhl(e)s**	**der Stühle**
dat	**dem Stuhl(e)**	**den Stühlen**

	singular	plural
nom	**die Angst**	**die Ängste**
acc	**die Angst**	**die Ängste**
gen	**der Angst**	**der Ängste**
dat	**der Angst**	**den Ängsten**

● Masculine and neuter nouns often add **-e** in the plural

	singular	plural
nom	**das Schicksal**	**die Schicksale**
acc	**das Schicksal**	**die Schicksale**
gen	**des Schicksals**	**der Schicksale**
dat	**dem Schicksal(e)**	**den Schicksalen**

● Masculine and neuter nouns sometimes add ⸚er or **-er**

	singular	plural
nom	**das Dach**	**die Dächer**
acc	**das Dach**	**die Dächer**
gen	**des Dach(e)s**	**der Dächer**
dat	**dem Dach(e)**	**den Dächern**

Continued

The Formation of Plurals (ctd.)

Some Unusual Plurals

das Ministerium, die Ministerien Department(s)
das Prinzip, die Prinzipien principle(s)
das Thema, die Themen theme(s), topic(s), subject(s)
das Drama, die Dramen drama(s)
die Firma, die Firmen firm(s)
das Konto, die Konten bank account(s)
das Risiko, die Risiken risk(s)
das Komma, die Kommas or **Kommata** comma(s); decimal point(s)
das Baby, die Babys baby (babies)
der Klub, die Klubs club(s)
der Streik, die Streiks strike(s)
der Park, die Parks park(s)
der Chef, die Chefs boss(es), chief(s), head(s)
der Israeli, die Israelis Israeli(s)
das Restaurant, die Restaurants restaurant(s)
das Bonbon, die Bonbons sweet(s)
das Hotel, die Hotels hotel(s)
das Niveau, die Niveaus standard(s), level(s)

German singular/English plural nouns

Some nouns are always plural in English, but singular in German:

● Some of the most common examples are:

  eine Brille glasses, spectacles
  eine Schere scissors
  eine Hose trousers

● They are only used in the plural in German to mean more than one pair, e.g. **zwei Hosen** *two pairs of trousers*

The Declension of Nouns (ctd.)

"Weak" Masculine nouns

Some masculine nouns have a weak declension, which means that in all cases apart from the nominative singular, they end in **-en** or, if the word ends in a vowel, in **-n**

- The dictionary will often show such nouns as
  Junge *m* **-n, -n** boy
  Held *m* **-en, -en** hero

- Weak masculine nouns are declined as follows:

	singular	plural
nom	der Junge	die Jungen
acc	den Jungen	die Jungen
gen	des Jungen	der Jungen
dat	dem Jungen	den Jungen

- Masculine nouns falling into this category include:
  — those ending in **-og(e)** referring to males:
    der Psychologe, der Geologe, der Astrologe
  — those ending in **-aph** or **-oph**:
    der Paragraph, der Philosoph
  — those ending in **-nom** referring to males:
    der Astronom, der Gastronom
  — those ending in **-ant**:
    der Elefant, der Diamant
  — those ending in **-t** which refer to males:
    der Astronaut, der Komponist, der Architekt
  — miscellaneous others:
    der Chirurg, der Bauer, der Ochs, der Kollege, der Spatz, der Mensch, der Katholik, der Franzose

- **der Name** (*name*) has a different ending in the genitive singular, **-ns**: **des Namens**. Otherwise it is the same as **der Junge** shown above. Others in this category are: **der Buchstabe, der Glaube, der Gedanke, der Haufe, der Funke**.

The Declension of Proper Nouns

- Names of people and places add **-s** in the genitive singular unless they are preceded by the definite article or a demonstrative (→1)

- Where proper names end in a sibilant (**-s, -sch, -ß, -x, -z, -tz**) and this makes the genitive form with **-s** almost impossible to pronounce, they are best avoided altogether by using **von** followed by the dative case (→2)

- Personal names can be given diminutive forms if desired. These may be used as a sign of affection as well as with diminutive meaning (→3)

- **Herr** (*Mr.*) is always declined where it occurs as part of a proper name (→4)

- When articles or adjectives form part of a proper name (e.g. in the names of books, plays, hotels, restaurants *etc*), these are declined in the normal way (see pp.118 and 140) (→5)

- Surnames usually form their plurals by adding **-s**, unless they end in a sibilant, in which case they sometimes add **-ens**. They are often preceded by the definite article (→6)

Nouns of Measurement and Quantity

- These usually remain singular, even if preceded by a plural number (→7)

- The substance which they measure follows in the same case as the noun of quantity, and not in the genitive case as in English (→8)

1   **Peters Buch** Peter's book
    Klaras Mantel Clara's coat
    Die Werke Goethes Goethe's works
    BUT: **die Versenkung der Bismarck**
    the sinking of the Bismarck

2   **Das Buch von Hans** Hans' book
    Die Werke von Marx The works of Marx
    Die Freundin von Klaus Klaus's girlfriend

3   **von Deinem Sabinchen** from your Sabine
    Das kleine Peterchen hat uns dann ein Lied gesungen
    Then little Peter sang us a song

4   **an Herrn Schmidt** to Mr. Smith
    Sehr geehrte Herren Dear sirs

5   **im Weißen Schwan** in the White Swan
    Er hat "Den Zauberberg" schon gelesen
    He has already read "The Magic Mountain"
    nach Karl dem Großen after Charlemagne

6   **Die Schmidts haben uns eingeladen**
    The Smiths have invited us
    Die Zeißens haben uns eingeladen
    Mr. and Mrs. Zeiß have invited us

7   **Möchten Sie zwei Stück?**
    Would you like two?

8   **Er wollte zwei Kilo Kartoffeln**
    He wanted two kilos of potatoes
    Sie hat drei Tassen Kaffee getrunken
    She drank three cups of coffee
    Drei Glas Weißwein, bitte!
    Three glasses of white wine please

The Definite Article

In English the definite article *the* always keeps the same form
    the book/*the* books/with *the* books
In German, however, the definite article has many forms:

- In its singular form it changes for masculine, feminine and neuter nouns (→1)

- In its plural forms, it is the same for all genders (→2)

- The definite article is also used to show the function of the noun in the sentence by showing which case it is.
There are four cases, as explained more fully on p.108:
    nominative for the subject or complement of the verb (→3)
    accusative for the object of the verb and after some prepositions (→4)
    genitive to show possession and after some prepositions (→5)
    dative for an indirect object (*to* or *for*) and after some prepositions and certain verbs (→6)

- The forms of the definite article are as follows:

| | singular | | | plural |
	masc	fem	neut	all genders
nom	der	die	das	die
acc	den	die	das	die
gen	des	der	des	der
dat	dem	der	dem	den (→7)

Continued

1 *masculine*:   **der Mann** the man
                der Wagen the car
  feminine: **die Frau** the wife/woman
                die Blume the flower
  neuter: **das Ding** the thing
                das Mädchen the girl

2 **die Männer/die Frauen/die Dinge**
the men/the women/the things

3 **Der Mann ist jung** The man is young
Die Frau/das Kind ist jung The woman/the child is young

4 **Ich kenne den Mann/die Frau/das Kind**
I know the man/the woman/the child

5 **der Kopf des Mannes/der Frau/des Kindes**
the man's/woman's/child's head
Wegen des Mannes/der Frau/des Kindes
Because of the man/the woman/the child

6 **Ich gab es dem Mann/der Frau/dem Kind**
I gave it to the man/to the woman/to the child

7

		singular	
	masc	fem	neut
nom	**der Mann**	**die Frau**	**das Kind**
acc	**den Mann**	**die Frau**	**das Kind**
gen	**des Mann(e)s**	**der Frau**	**des Kind(e)s**
dat	**dem Mann(e)**	**der Frau**	**dem Kind(e)**

		plural	
	masc	fem	neut
nom	**die Männer**	**die Frauen**	**die Kinder**
acc	**die Männer**	**die Frauen**	**die Kinder**
gen	**der Männer**	**der Frauen**	**der Kinder**
dat	**den Männern**	**den Frauen**	**den Kindern**

Uses of the Definite Article

When to use and when not to use the definite article in German is one of the most difficult areas for the learner. The following guidelines show where German practice varies from English.

The definite article is used with:

- abstract and other nouns where something is being referred to as a whole or as a general idea (→**1**)
  Where these nouns are quantified or modified, the article is not used (→**2**)

- the genitive, unless the noun is a proper name or is acting as a proper name (→**3**)

- occasionally with proper names to make the sex or case clearer (→**4**)

- always with proper names preceded by an adjective (→**5**)

- sometimes with proper names in familiar contexts or for slight emphasis (→**6**)

- with masculine and feminine countries and districts (→**7**)

- with geographical names preceded by an adjective (→**8**)

- with names of seasons (→**9**)

- often with meals (→**10**)

- with the names of roads (→**11**)

Continued

1 Das Leben ist schön Life is wonderful
2 Es braucht Mut It needs (some) courage
  Gibt es dort Leben? Is there (any) life there?
3 Das Auto des Lehrers The teacher's car
  Peters Auto Peter's car
  Muttis Auto Mummy's car
4 Er hat es Frau Lehmann gegeben
  Er hat es der Frau Lehmann gegeben
  He gave it to Frau Lehmann
5 Der alte Herr Brockhaus ist damals sehr taub gewesen
  Old Mr. Brockhaus went very deaf at that time
6 Ich habe heute den Peter gesehen
  I saw Peter today
  Du hast es aber nicht der Petra geschenkt!
  You haven't given it to *Petra*!
7 Deutschland ist sehr schön Germany is very beautiful
  Die Schweiz ist auch schön Switzerland is also lovely
8 Im (= in dem) heutigen Deutschland
  In today's Germany
9 Im (= in dem) Sommer gehen wir schwimmen
  We go swimming in summer
  Der Winter kommt bald
  Soon it will be winter
10 Das Abendessen wird ab acht Uhr serviert
  Dinner is served from eight o'clock
  Was gibt's zum (= zu dem) Mittagessen?
  What's for lunch?
  BUT
  Um 8 Uhr ist Frühstück
  Breakfast is at 8 o'clock
11 Sie wohnt jetzt in der Geisenerstraße
  She lives in Geisener Road now

Uses of the Definite Article (ctd.)

- with months of the year except after **seit/nach/vor** (→**1**)

- instead of the possessive adjective to refer to parts of the body and items of clothing (→**2**)
  A reflexive pronoun or noun in the dative case is used if it is necessary to clarify to whom the parts of the body belong (→**3**)

- in expressions of price, to mean *each/per/a* (→**4**)

- with certain common expressions (→**5**)

Other Uses

- The definite article can be used with demonstrative meaning (→**6**)

- After certain prepositions, forms of the definite article can be shortened (see p.198 ff).
  Some of these forms are best used in informal situations (→**7**)
  Others are commonly and correctly used in formal contexts (→**8, 1, 5**)

The definite article may be omitted in German:

- in certain set expressions (→**9**)

- in *preposition + adjective + noun* combinations (→**10**)
  For the declension of adjectives without the article see p.142.

1 Wir fahren im (= in dem) September weg
   We are going away in September
   Wir sind seit September hier
   We have been here since September

2 Er legte den Hut auf den Tisch
   He laid his hat on the table
   Ich drücke die Daumen I'm keeping my fingers crossed

3 Er hat sich die Hände schon gewaschen
   He has already washed his hands
   Er hat dem Kind schon die Hände gewaschen
   He has already washed the child's hands

4 Die kosten ...   They cost ...
   ... fünf Mark das Pfund   ... five marks a pound
   ... sechs Mark das Stück   ... six marks each

5 in die Stadt fahren to go into town
   zur (= zu der) Schule gehen to go to school
   mit der Post by post
   mit dem Zug/Bus/Auto by train/bus/car
   im (= in dem) Gefängnis in prison

6 Du willst das Buch lesen!
   You want to read *that* book!

7 für das → fürs; vor dem → vorm; um das → ums *etc*

8 an dem → am; zu dem → zum; zu der → zur *etc*

9 von Beruf by profession
   nach Wunsch as desired
   mit Kind und Kegel with bag and baggage
   Nachrichten hören to listen to the news

10 Mit gebeugtem Rücken, ... Bending his back, ...

The Indefinite Article

Like the definite article, the form of the indefinite article
varies depending on the gender and case of the noun (→**1**)
It has no plural forms (→**2**)

The indefinite article is declined as follows:

	masc	fem	neut	
nom	**ein**	**eine**	**ein**	
acc	**einen**	**eine**	**ein**	
gen	**eines**	**einer**	**eines**	
dat	**einem**	**einer**	**einem**	(→**3**)

● The indefinite article is omitted in the following:

— descriptions of people by profession, religion,
  nationality etc (→**4**)
  But note that the article is included when an adjective
  precedes the noun (→**5**)

— in certain fixed expressions (→**6**)

— after **als** *as a* (→**7**)

1 **Da ist ein Auto** There's a car
    Er hat eine Wohnung He has a flat
    Sie gab es einem Kind She gave it to a child

2 **Autos sind in letzter Zeit teurer geworden**
    Cars have become more expensive recently

3

	MASC	SINGULAR FEM	NEUT
NOM	**ein Mann**	**eine Frau**	**ein Kind**
ACC	**einen Mann**	**eine Frau**	**ein Kind**
GEN	**eines Mann(e)s**	**einer Frau**	**eines Kind(e)s**
DAT	**einem Mann(e)**	**einer Frau**	**einem Kind(e)**

4 **Sie ist Kinderärztin** She's a paediatrician
    Sie ist Deutsche She's (a) German

5 **Sie ist eine sehr geschickte Kinderärztin**
    She's a very clever paediatrician

6 **Es ist Geschmacksache** It's a question of taste
    Tatsache ist ...   It's a fact ...
    Ich habe Kopfschmerzen I've got a headache

7 **Als Ausländer ist er hier nicht wahlberechtigt**
    As a foreigner he doesn't have the vote here
    ... und ich rede nun als Vater von vier Kindern
    ... and I'm talking now as a father of four

Words declined like the Definite Article

The following have endings similar to those of the definite article shown on p.118:

> **jeder, jede, jedes** each, each one, every
> **jener, jene, jenes** that, that one, those
> **dieser, diese, dieses** this, this one, these
> **solcher, solche, solches** such/such a
> **sämtliche** all, entire (*usually plural*)
> **mancher, manche, manches** many a/some
> **einiger, einige, einiges** some, a few, a little
> **welcher, welche, welches** which, which one
> **aller, alle, alles** all, all of them
> **irgendwelcher, -e, -es** some or other
> **beide** both (*plural only*)

● These words can be used as: articles (→1)
                                     pronouns (→2)

● They have the following endings:

	singular			plural
	masc	fem	neut	all genders
nom	-er	-e	-es	-e
acc	-en	-e	-es	-e
gen	-es/-en	-er	-es/-en	-er
dat	-em	-er	-em	-en

Example declensions are shown on p.134ff.

● **einiger** and **irgendwelcher** use the **-en** genitive ending before masculine or neuter nouns ending in **-s** (→3)
jeder, welcher, mancher and **solcher** may also do so (→4)

Continued

1 Dieser Mann kommt aus Südamerika
This man comes from South America
Er geht jeden Tag ins Büro
He goes to the office every day
Manche Leute können das nicht
A good many people can't do it

2 Willst du diesen? Do you want this one?
In manchem hat er recht He's right about some things
Man kann ja nicht alles wissen
You can't know everything
Es gibt manche, die keinen Alkohol mögen
There are some people who don't like alcohol

3 wegen irgendwelchen Streites
on account of some argument or other

4 der Besitz solchen Reichtums
the possession of such wealth
trotz jeden Versuchs
despite all attempts

Words declined like the Definite Article
(ctd.)

- Adjectives following these words have the weak declension
  (see p.140) (→1)
  Exceptions are the plural forms of **einige**, which are
  followed by the strong declension (see p.142) (→2)

Further points

- **solcher, beide, sämtliche** may be used after another
  article or possessive adjective. They then take weak (see
  p.140) or mixed (see p.142) adjectival endings, as
  appropriate (→3)

- Although **beide** generally has plural forms only, one
  singular form does exist. This is in the neuter nominative
  and accusative: **beides** (→4)

- **dies** often replaces the nominative and accusative **dieses**
  and **diese** when used as a pronoun (→5)

- **alles** as the genitive singular of the pronoun **aller** is used
  with the demonstrative **das** (→6)

- A fixed form **all** exists which is used together with other
  articles or possessive pronouns (→7)

- **ganz** can also be used to replace both the inflected form
  aller/alle/alles and the uninflected **all das/dieses/sein**
  etc.
  It is declined as a normal adjective (see p. 140) (→8)
  It must be used with collective nouns, in time phrases and
  geographical references (→9)

Continued

1   **dieses alte Auto** this old car
    aus irgendwelchem dummen Grunde
    for some stupid reason or other
    welche neuen Waren? which new goods?

2   **Die sind einige gute Freunde von mir**
    These are some good friends of mine

3   **Ein solches Kleid habe ich früher auch getragen**
    I used to wear a dress like that too
    Diese beiden Männer haben es gesehen
    Both of these men have seen it

4   **Beides ist richtig** Both are right
    Sie hat beides genommen She took both

5   **Hast du dies schon gelesen?**
    Have you already read this?
    Dies sind meine neuen Sachen
    These are my new things

6   **Der Besitzer alles, das wir gerade besichtigt hatten ...**
    The owner of everything that we had just looked at ...

7   **All sein Mut war verschwunden**
    All his courage had vanished
    mit all diesem Geld   with all this money

8   **mit dem ganzen Geld** with all this money

9   **die ganze Gesellschaft** the entire company
    Es hat den ganzen Tag geschneit
    It snowed the whole day long
    Im ganzen Land gab es kein besseres
    There wasn't a better one in the whole country

Words declined like the Definite Article
(ctd.)

- **derjenige/diejenige/dasjenige** (*the one, those*) is declined exactly as the definite article plus an adjective in the weak declension (see p.140) (→**1**)

- **derselbe/dieselbe/dasselbe** (*the same, the same one*) is declined in the same way as **derjenige** (→**2**)

  After prepositions however, the normal contracted forms of the definite article are used for the appropriate parts of **derselbe** (→**3**)

Continued

1

SINGULAR

MASC	FEM	NEUT
derjenige Mann	diejenige Frau	dasjenige Kind
denjenigen Mann	diejenige Frau	dasjenige Kind
desjenigen Mann(e)s	derjenigen Frau	desjenigen Kind(e)s
demjenigen Mann(e)	derjenigen Frau	demjenigen Kind(e)

PLURAL

MASC	FEM	NEUT
diejenigen Männer	diejenigen Frauen	diejenigen Kinder
diejenigen Männer	diejenigen Frauen	diejenigen Kinder
derjenigen Männer	derjenigen Frauen	derjenigen Kinder
denjenigen Männern	denjenigen Frauen	denjenigen Kindern

2

SINGULAR

MASC	FEM	NEUT
derselbe Mann	dieselbe Frau	dasselbe Kind
denselben Mann	dieselbe Frau	dasselbe Kind
desselben Mann(e)s	derselben Frau	desselben Kind(e)s
demselben Mann(e)	derselben Frau	demselben Kind(e)

PLURAL

MASC	FEM	NEUT
dieselben Männer	dieselben Frauen	dieselben Kinder
dieselben Männer	dieselben Frauen	dieselben Kinder
derselben Männer	derselben Frauen	derselben Kinder
denselben Männern	denselben Frauen	denselben Kindern

3 zur selben (= zu derselben) **Zeit** at the same time
im selben (= in demselben) **Zimmer** in the same room

Words declined like the Definite Article
(ctd.)

Sample Declensions in full

dieser, diese, dieses this, this one

SINGULAR

	MASC	FEM	NEUT
nom	dieser Mann	diese Frau	dieses Kind
acc	diesen Mann	diese Frau	dieses Kind
gen	dieses Mann(e)s	dieser Frau	dieses Kind(e)s
dat	diesem Mann(e)	dieser Frau	diesem Kind(e)

PLURAL

	MASC	FEM	NEUT
nom	diese Männer	diese Frauen	diese Kinder
acc	diese Männer	diese Frauen	diese Kinder
gen	dieser Männer	dieser Frauen	dieser Kinder
dat	diesen Männern	diesen Frauen	diesen Kindern

jener, jene, jenes that, that one

SINGULAR

	MASC	FEM	NEUT
nom	jener Mann	jene Frau	jenes Kind
acc	jenen Mann	jene Frau	jenes Kind
gen	jenes Mann(e)s	jener Frau	jenes Kind(e)s
dat	jenem Mann(e)	jener Frau	jenem Kind(e)

PLURAL

	MASC	FEM	NEUT
nom	jene Männer	jene Frauen	jene Kinder
acc	jene Männer	jene Frauen	jene Kinder
gen	jener Männer	jener Frauen	jener Kinder
dat	jenen Männern	jenen Frauen	jenen Kindern

jeder, jede, jedes each, every, everybody

	MASC	SINGULAR FEM	NEUT
nom	jeder Wagen	jede Minute	jedes Bild
acc	jeden Wagen	jede Minute	jedes Bild
gen	jedes Wagens	jeder Minute	jedes Bild(e)s
	(jeden Wagens)		(jeden Bild(e)s)
dat	jedem Wagen	jeder Minute	jedem Bild(e)

welcher, welche, welches which?, which

	MASC	SINGULAR FEM	NEUT
nom	welcher Preis	welche Sorte	welches Mädchen
acc	welchen Preis	welche Sorte	welches Mädchen
gen	welches Preises	welcher Sorte	welches Mädchens
	(welchen Preises)		(welchen Mädchens)
dat	welchem Preis	welcher Sorte	welchem Mädchen

	MASC	PLURAL FEM	NEUT
nom	welche Preise	welche Sorten	welche Mädchen
acc	welche Preise	welche Sorten	welche Mädchen
gen	welcher Preise	welcher Sorten	welcher Mädchen
dat	welchen Preisen	welchen Sorten	welchen Mädchen

Words declined like the Indefinite Article

The following have the same declension pattern as the indefinite articles **ein** and **kein** (see pp.124 and 126):

The possessive adjectives

mein my (→**1**)
dein your (*singular familiar*)
sein his/its
ihr her/its (→**2**)
unser our
euer your (*plural familiar*)
ihr their (→**2**)
Ihr your (*polite singular and plural*)

These words are declined as follows:

| | singular | | | plural |
	masc	fem	neut	all genders
nom	—	-e	—	-e
acc	-en	-e	—	-e
gen	-es	-er	-es	-er
dat	-em	-er	-em	-en

- Adjectives following these determiners have the mixed declension forms (see p.142), e.g.:

    sein altes Auto   his old car

- **irgendein** *some ... or other* also follows this declension pattern in the singular.
  Its plural form is **irgendwelche** (see p.128).

1 **Das Buch ist neu** The book is new
Der Vortrag war sehr langweilig
The lecture was very boring

2 **Das neue Buch ist da** The new book has arrived
Während des langweiligen Vortrags sind wir alle eingeschlafen
We all fell asleep during the boring lecture

3 **der junge Rechtsanwalt** the young lawyer
ein junger Rechtsanwalt a young lawyer
manch junger Rechtsanwalt many a young lawyer

4

| | SINGULAR | |
	MASC	FEM	NEUT
nom	**der alte Mann**	**die alte Frau**	**das alte Haus**
acc	**den alten Mann**	**die alte Frau**	**das alte Haus**
gen	**des alten Mann(e)s**	**der alten Frau**	**des alten Hauses**
dat	**dem alten Mann(e)**	**der alten Frau**	**dem alten Haus(e)**

| | PLURAL | |
	MASC	FEM	NEUT
nom	**die alten Männer**	**die alten Frauen**	**die alten Häuser**
acc	**die alten Männer**	**die alten Frauen**	**die alten Häuser**
gen	**der alten Männer**	**der alten Frauen**	**der alten Häuser**
dat	**den alten Männern**	**den alten Frauen**	**den alten Häusern**

The Declension of Adjectives (ctd.)

2 The mixed declension

These are the endings used after **ein, kein, irgendein** and the possessive adjectives (see p.136) (→**1**):

	singular			plural
	masc	fem	neut	all genders
nom	-er	-e	-es	-en
acc	-en	-e	-es	-en
gen	-en	-en	-en	-en
dat	-en	-en	-en	-en (→**2**)

3 The strong declension

Strong declension endings:

	singular			plural
	masc	fem	neut	all genders
nom	-er	-e	-es	-e
acc	-en	-e	-es	-e
gen	-en	-er	-en	-er
dat	-em	-er	-em	-en (→**3**)

These endings are used where there is no preceding article. The article is omitted more frequently in German than in English, especially in combinations "preposition + adjective + noun" (see p.122).

These endings enable the adjective to do the work of the missing article by showing case, number and gender (→**4**)

Continued

1 **Meine neue Stelle ist bei einer großen Druckerei**
My new job is with a large printing works
Ihre frühere Theorie ist jetzt bestätigt worden
Her earlier theory has now been proved true

2

	SINGULAR	
MASC	FEM	NEUT
ein langer Weg	eine lange Reise	ein langes Spiel
einen langen Weg	eine lange Reise	ein langes Spiel
eines langen Wegs	einer langen Reise	eines langen Spieles
einem langen Weg	einer langen Reise	einem langen Spiel

PLURAL
ALL GENDERS

nom	ihre langen Wege / Reisen / Spiele
acc	ihre langen Wege / Reisen / Spiele
gen	ihrer langen Wege / Reisen / Spiele
dat	ihren langen Wegen / Reisen / Spielen

3

	SINGULAR		
	MASC	FEM	NEUT
nom	guter Käse	gute Marmelade	gutes Bier
acc	guten Käse	gute Marmelade	gutes Bier
gen	guten Käses	guter Marmelade	guten Biers
dat	gutem Käse	guter Marmelade	gutem Bier

PLURAL
ALL GENDERS

nom	gute Käse / Marmeladen / Biere
acc	gute Käse / Marmeladen / Biere
gen	guter Käse / Marmeladen / Biere
dat	guten Käsen / Marmeladen / Bieren

4 **nach kurzer Fahrt** after a short journey
mit gleichem Gehalt with the same salary

The Declension of Adjectives (ctd.)

- Strong declension endings are also used after any of the following where they are not preceded by an article or other determiner:

  ein bißchen a little, a bit of
  ein wenig a little
  ein paar a few, a couple (→1)
  weniger fewer, less
  einige (*plural forms only*) some
  allerlei/allerhand all kinds of, all sorts of
  keinerlei no ... whatsoever, no ... at all
  mancherlei various, a number of
  etwas some, any (*singular*) (→2)
  mehr more
  lauter nothing but, sheer, pure
  solch such
  vielerlei various, all sorts of, many different
  mehrerlei several kinds of
  was für what, what kind of
  (*note that* **was für ein** *takes the mixed declension*)
  welcherlei what kind of, what sort of
  viel much, many, a lot of
  wievielerlei how many kinds of
  welch! what! what a! (→3)
  manch many a
  wenig little, few, not much (→4)
  zweierlei/dreierlei *etc* two/three *etc* kinds of
  zwei, drei *etc* two, three *etc* (→5)
  (*but note that the mixed declension is used after* **ein**)

- The strong declension is also required after possessives where no other word indicates the case, gender and number (→6)

Continued

1 **ein paar gute Tips** (*strong declension*)
   a couple of good tips

2 **Etwas starken Pfeffer zugeben** (*strong*)
   Add a little strong pepper

3 **Welch herrliches Wetter!** (*strong*)
   What splendid weather!

4 **Es gab damals nur wenig frisches Obst** (*strong*)
   At that time there was little fresh fruit
   BUT
   Das wenige frische Obst, das es damals gab ... (*weak*)
   The little fresh fruit that was then available ...

5 **Zwei große Jungen waren herangekommen** (*strong*)
   Two big boys had come along
   BUT
   Die zwei großen Jungen, die herangekommen waren (*weak*)
   The two big boys who had come along
   Meine zwei großen Jungen (*mixed*)
   My two big sons

6 **Peters altes Buch** (*strong*)
   Peter's old book

   Muttis neues Auto (*strong*)
   Mum's new car

The Declension of Adjectives (ctd.)

Some spelling changes when adjectives are declined

- When the adjective **hoch** (*high*) is declined, its stem changes to **hoh-** (→1)

- Adjectives ending in **-el** lose the **-e** of their stem when inflected, i.e. when endings are added (→2)

- Adjectives with an **-er** ending often lose the **-e** from the ending when inflected (→3)

The participles as adjectives

- The present participle can be used as an adjective with normal adjectival endings (pp.140 to 143) (→4)
  The present participles of **sein** and **haben** cannot be used in this way

- The past participle can also be used as an adjective in this way (→5)

Adjectives followed by the dative case

A *dative case* is required after many adjectives e.g. (→6):
  ähnlich similar to
  bekannt familiar to
  dankbar grateful to
  fremd alien to
  gleich all the same to; like
  leicht easy for
  nah close to
  peinlich painful for
  unbekannt unknown to

1 Das Gebäude ist hoch The building is high
BUT
ein hohes Gebäude a high building

2 Das Zimmer ist dunkel The room is dark
BUT
in dem dunklen Zimmer in the dark room

3 Das Auto war teuer The car was expensive
BUT
Er kaufte ein teures Auto He bought an expensive car

4 die werdende Mutter the mother-to-be
ein lachendes Kind a laughing child

5 meine verlorenen Sachen my lost things
die ausgebeuteten Arbeiter
the exploited workers

6 Ist dir das bekannt? Do you know about it?
Ich wäre Ihnen dankbar, wenn ...
I should be grateful to you if ...
Diese Sache ist mir etwas peinlich
This matter is somewhat embarrassing for me
Solche Gedanken waren ihm fremd
Such thoughts were alien to him

Adjectives used as nouns

All adjectives in German, and those participles used as adjectives, can also be used as nouns. These are often called **adjectival nouns**.

- Adjectives and participles used as nouns have:
  a capital letter like other nouns (→1)
  declension endings like other adjectives, depending on the preceding article, if any (see below) (→2)

Declension endings for adjectives used as nouns:

- after **der, dieser** and words like it shown on p.128, the normal *weak* adjective endings apply (see p.140) (→3)
  Der Junge (*the boy*) is an exception and is declined like a weak masculine noun, as shown on p.115.

- after **ein, kein, irgendein** and the possessive adjectives shown on p.136, the *mixed* adjective endings apply (see p.142) (→4)

- where no article is present, or after those words shown on p.144, the *strong* adjective endings are used (see p.142) (→5)
  When another adjective precedes the adjectival noun, the *strong* endings become *weak* in two instances:

  in the *dative singular* (→6)

  in the *nominative and accusative plural* after a possessive, where the strong endings might cause confusion with the singular feminine form (→7)

- Some adjectival nouns have become part of set expressions, and these tend to be written without the capital letter (→8)

1 **der Angestellte** the employee

2 **die Angestellte** the female employee
das Neue daran ist ... the new thing about it is ...

3 **für den Angeklagten** for the accused
mit dieser Bekannten with this (*female*) friend

4 **Kein Angestellter darf hier rauchen**
No employee may smoke here
Sie machten einen Ausflug mit ihren Bekannten zusammen
They went on a trip with their friends

5 **Etwas Besonderes ist geschehen**
Something special has happened

6 **Ich hatte es Peters jüngerem Verwandten versprochen**
I had promised it to Peter's young relative

7 **Peters jüngere Verwandten wollten es haben**
Peter's young relatives wanted to have it

8 **Es bleibt beim alten** Things remain as they were
Er hat den ersten besten genommen
He took the first that came to hand

Miscellaneous points

Adjectives of nationality

- These are not spelt with a capital letter in German except in public or official names (→1)

- However, when used as a noun to refer to the language, a capital is used (→2)

- In German, for expressions like *he is English*/*he is German etc* a noun or adjectival noun is used instead of an adjective (→3)

Adjectives derived from place names

- These are formed by adding **-er** to names of towns (→4)

- They are never inflected (→5)

- Adjectives from **die Schweiz** and from certain regions can also be formed in this way (→6)

- Such adjectives may be used as nouns denoting the inhabitants of a town.
  They are then declined as normal nouns (see p.98ff) (→7)
  The feminine form is made by adding **-in** in the singular and **-innen** in the plural (→8)

- Certain names ending in **-en** drop the **-e** or the **-en** of their ending before adding **-er** (→9)

- A second type of adjective formed from place names exists, ending in **-isch** and spelt with a small letter. It is inflected as a normal adjective (see p.140).
  It is used mainly where the speaker is referring to the mood of, or something typical of that place (→10)

1 **Die deutsche Sprache** the German language
Das französische Volk The French people
BUT **Die Deutsche Schlaf- und Speisewagen Gesellschaft**

2 **Sie sprechen kein Englisch** They don't speak English

3 **Er ist Deutscher** He is German
Sie ist Deutsche She is German

4 **Kölner, Frankfurter, Düsseldorfer** *etc*

5 **der Kölner Dom** Cologne cathedral
ein Frankfurter Würstchen a frankfurter sausage

6 **Schweizer Käse** Swiss cheese

7 **Die Sprache des Kölners heißt Kölsch**
Von den Frankfurtern ...

8 **Die Kölnerin, die Kölnerinnen**
Die Londonerin, die Londonerinnen

9 **München** → **der Münchner**
Bremen → **der Bremer**
Göttingen → **der Göttinger**

10 **Ein richtig frankfurterischer Ausdruck**
A real Frankfurt expression
Er spricht etwas münchnerisch
He has something of a Munich accent

The Comparison of Adjectives

Adjectives have three basic forms of comparison:

A simple form used to describe something or someone:

e.g. a *little* house/the house is *little*

- This form is fully dealt with on pp. 140 to 147.

- Simple forms are used in *as ... as* / *not as ... as* comparisons (→1)

A comparative form used to compare two things or persons:

e.g. he is *bigger* than his brother

- In German, comparatives are formed by adding **-er** to the simple form (→2)

- *than* in comparative statements is translated by **als** (→3)

- Unlike English, the vast majority of German adjectives, including those of several syllables, form their comparatives in this way (→4)

- Many adjectives modify the stem vowel when forming their comparatives, as in the common examples shown opposite (→5)

Continued

1 **so ... wie** as ... as:
Er ist so gut wie sein Bruder
He is as good as his brother

ebenso ... wie just as ... as:
Er war ebenso glücklich wie ich
He was just as happy as I was

zwei/dreimal *etc* **so ... wie**
twice/three *etc* times as ... as:
Er war zweimal so groß wie sein Bruder
He was twice as big as his brother

nicht so ... wie not as ... as:
Er ist nicht so alt wie du
He is not as old as you

2 **klein / kleiner**   small / smaller
   schön / schöner   lovely / lovelier

3 **Er ist kleiner als seine Schwester**
He is smaller than his sister

4 **bequem / bequemer**   comfortable / more comfortable
   gebildet / gebildeter   educated / more educated
   effektiv / effektiver   effective / more effective

5 **alt / älter**   old / older
   stark / stärker   strong / stronger
   schwach / schwächer   weak / weaker
   scharf / schärfer   sharp / sharper
   lang / länger   long / longer
   kurz / kürzer   short / shorter
   warm / wärmer   warm / warmer
   kalt / kälter   cold / colder
   hart / härter   hard / harder
   groß / größer   big / bigger

Comparison of Adjectives (ctd.)

- Adjectives whose simple form ends in **-el** lose the **-e-** before adding the comparative ending **-er** (→1)

- Adjectives with a diphthong followed by **-er** in their simple forms also drop the **-e-** before adding **-er** (→2)

- Adjectives whose simple form ends in **-en** or **-er** may drop the **-e-** of the simple form when adjectival endings are added to their comparative forms (→3)

- With a few adjectives, comparative forms may be used not only for comparison, but also to render the idea of "-ish" or "rather ..."
  Some common examples are:

älter elderly	**dünner** thinnish
größer largish	**kürzer** shortish
kleiner smallish	**jünger** youngish
dicker fattish	**neuer** newish (→4)

- When used attributively (*before* the noun), comparative forms are declined in exactly the same way as simple adjectives (see pp.140 to 147) (→4, 5)

A superlative form used to compare three or more persons or things:

  e.g. he is *the biggest/the best*

- Superlatives are formed by adding **-st** to the simple adjective. The vowel is modified, as for comparative forms, where applicable.
  Superlative forms are generally used with an article and take endings accordingly (see p. 140) (→6)

Continued

1 **Der Tisch** the table (*masculine*)
Die Gardine the curtain (*feminine*)
Das Baby the baby (*neuter*)

2 **Das Bild ist schön**   → **Es ist schön**
The picture is beautiful   → It is beautiful

3 **Der Tisch ist groß**   → **Er ist groß**
The table is large   → It is large

4 **Die Gardine ist weiß**   → **Sie ist weiß**
The curtain is white   → It is white

5 **Das Kind stand auf**   → **Es stand auf**
The child stood up   → He/she stood up

6 **Es tut einem gut** It does one good

7 **Man holt mich um sieben ab**
I am being picked up at seven

8			
meiner	of me	**unser**	of us
deiner	of you	**euer**	of you (*plural*)
seiner	of him/of it	**ihrer**	of them
ihrer	of her/it	**Ihrer**	of you (*polite*)

9 **meinetwegen** because of me, on my account
deinetwegen because of you, on your account *etc*
seinetwegen
ihretwegen
unsertwegen
euretwegen
Ihretwegen

meinetwillen for my sake, for me *etc*
deinetwillen
ihretwillen *etc*

Personal Pronouns (ctd.)

The use of pronouns after prepositions

- Personal pronouns used after prepositions and referring to a person are in the *case* required by the preposition in question (see p.198ff) (→1)

- When, however, a *thing* rather than a person is referred to, the construction:

  preposition + pronoun

  becomes:

  da- + *preposition* (→2) Before a preposition beginning with a vowel, the form: **dar-** + *preposition* is used (→3)

  This affects the following prepositions:

an	auf	aus
bei	durch	für
in	mit	nach
neben	über	unter
zwischen		

- These contracted forms are used after verbs followed by a preposition (see p.76ff) (→4)

- After prepositions used to express motion the form with **da(r)-** is not felt to be sufficiently strong. Forms with **hin** and **her** are used as follows:

  aus : heraus / hinaus
  auf : herauf / hinauf
  in : herein / hinein (→4)

1 Ich bin mit ihm spazierengegangen
   I went for a walk with him

**2 Klaus hatte ein Messer geholt und wollte damit den Kuchen
   aufschneiden**
   Klaus had brought a knife and was about to slice the cake with it

3 Lege es bitte darauf
   Put it on there please

4 Der Unterschied liegt darin, daß ...
   The difference is that ...
   Ich erinnere mich nicht daran
   I don't remember (it)

5 Er sah eine Treppe und ging leise hinauf
   He saw some stairs and climbed them quietly
   Endlich fand er unser Zelt und kam herein
   He finally found our tent and came in
   Er öffnete den Koffer und legte das Hemd hinein
   He opened his suitcase and put in his shirt

Possessive Pronouns

meiner mine
deiner yours
seiner his/its
ihrer hers/its
uns(e)rer ours
eu(e)rer yours (*plural*)
ihrer theirs
Ihrer yours (*polite form*)

These have the same endings as **dieser**. Their declension is therefore the same as for possessive adjectives (see p. 136) except in the masculine nominative singular and the neuter nominative and accusative singular:

	singular			plural
	masc	fem	neut	all genders
nom	**-ER**	**-e**	**-(E)S**	**-e**
acc	**-en**	**-e**	**-(E)S**	**-e**
gen	**-es**	**-er**	**-es**	**-er**
dat	**-em**	**-er**	**-em**	**-en**

- The bracketed **(e)** is often omitted, especially in spoken German

- Possessive pronouns must agree in number, gender and case with the noun they replace (→1)

- Note the translation of *of mine, of yours* etc (→2)

- **meiner** is declined in full opposite (→3)
  Like **meiner** are **deiner**, **seiner** and **ihrer**.
  Unserer and **euerer** are shown in full, since they have slightly different forms with an optional **-e-** (→4)

Continued

1 Der Wagen da drüben ist meiner. Er ist kleiner als deiner
The car over there is mine. It is smaller than yours

2 Er ist ein Bekannter von mir
He is an acquaintance of mine

3 meiner mine

	SINGULAR		PLURAL
MASC	FEM	NEUT	ALL GENDERS
meiner	**meine**	**mein(e)s**	**meine**
meinen	**meine**	**mein(e)s**	**meine**
meines	**meiner**	**meines**	**meiner**
meinem	**meiner**	**meinem**	**meinen**

4 uns(e)rer ours

	SINGULAR		PLURAL
MASC	FEM	NEUT	ALL GENDERS
uns(e)rer	**uns(e)re**	**uns(e)res**	**uns(e)re**
uns(e)ren	**uns(e)re**	**uns(e)res**	**uns(e)re**
uns(e)res	**uns(e)rer**	**uns(e)res**	**uns(e)rer**
uns(e)rem	**uns(e)rer**	**uns(e)rem**	**uns(e)ren**

eu(e)rer yours (*plural*)

	SINGULAR		PLURAL
MASC	FEM	NEUT	ALL GENDERS
eu(e)rer	**eu(e)re**	**euer(e)s**	**eu(e)re**
eu(e)ren	**eu(e)re**	**euer(e)s**	**eu(e)re**
eu(e)res	**eu(e)rer**	**eu(e)res**	**eu(e)rer**
eu(e)rem	**eu(e)rer**	**eu(e)rem**	**eu(e)ren**

Possessive Pronouns (ctd.)

Alternative forms

There are two alternatives to the **meiner/deiner** *etc* forms
shown on p.167:

- **der, die, das meinige** mine
  der, die, das deinige yours
  der, die, das seinige his/its
  der, die, das ihrige hers/its
  der, die, das uns(e)rige ours
  der, die, das eu(e)rige yours (*plural*)
  der, die, das ihrige theirs
  der, die, das Ihrige yours (*polite form*)

These are almost as common as the **meiner/deiner** *etc*
forms (→**1**)

These forms are declined as the definite article plus a weak
adjective (see p.140) (→**2**)

The bracketed (**e**) of the first and second person plural is
often omitted in spoken German.

- **der, die, das meine** mine
  der, die, das deine yours
  der, die, das seine his/its
  der, die, das ihre hers/its
  der, die, das uns(e)re ours
  der, die, das eu(e)re yours (*plural*)
  der, die, das ihre theirs
  der, die, das Ihre yours (*polite form*)

These forms are not as widely used as either of the previous
two forms. They are declined as the definite article followed
by a weak adjective (→**3**)

1   **Ihr Auto ist aber neuer als das meinige**
Your car is newer than mine
Paul hat seiner Freundin Blumen gekauft. Ich habe der meinigen Parfüm geschenkt
Paul bought his girlfriend some flowers. I bought mine perfume

2

	SINGULAR	
MASC	FEM	NEUT
der meinige	die meinige	das meinige
den meinigen	die meinige	das meinige
des meinigen	der meinigen	des meinigen
dem meinigen	der meinigen	dem meinigen

PLURAL
ALL GENDERS
die meinigen
die meinigen
der meinigen
den meinigen

3

	SINGULAR	
MASC	FEM	NEUT
der meine	die meine	das meine
den meinen	die meine	das meine
des meinen	der meinen	des meinen
dem meinen	der meinen	dem meinen

PLURAL
ALL GENDERS
die meinen
die meinen
der meinen
den meinen

Reflexive Pronouns

Reflexive pronouns, used to form reflexive verbs, have two forms, accusative and dative, as follows (→1)

ACCUSATIVE	DATIVE	
mich	**mir**	myself
dich	**dir**	yourself
sich	**sich**	himself/herself/ itself/themselves
uns	**uns**	ourselves
euch	**euch**	yourselves
sich	**sich**	yourself/yourselves (*polite forms*)

● Unlike personal pronouns and possessives, the polite forms have no capital letter (→2)

● For the position of reflexive pronouns within a sentence see p.30 (reflexive verbs) and pp.224 to 235 (sentence structure).

● Reflexive pronouns are also used after prepositions when the pronoun has the function of "reflecting back" to the subject of the sentence (→3)

● A further use of reflexive pronouns in German is with transitive verbs where the action is performed for the benefit of the subject, as in the English phrase:

I bought *myself* a new hat

The pronoun is not always translated in English (→4)

Continued

1 **Er hat sich rasiert** He had a shave
   Wir haben uns gebadet We had a bath
   Ich will es mir zuerst überlegen
   I'll have to think about it first

2 **Setzen Sie sich, bitte** Please take a seat

3 **Er hatte nicht genug Geld bei sich** (NOT **bei ihm**)
   He didn't have enough money on him

4 **Ich hole mir ein Bier**
   I'm going to get a beer (for myself)
   Er hat sich einen neuen Anzug gekauft
   He bought (himself) a new suit

Reflexive Pronouns (ctd.)

● Reflexive pronouns may be used for *reciprocal* actions, usually rendered by "each other" in English (→**1**)

Reciprocal actions may also be expressed by **einander**. This does not change in form (→**2**)

einander is always used in place of the reflexive pronoun after prepositions. Note that the preposition and **einander** come together to form one word (→**3**)

Emphatic reflexive pronouns

In English, these have the same forms as the normal reflexive pronouns:

The queen *herself* has given the order
I haven't read it *myself*, but ...

In German, this idea is expressed not by the reflexive pronouns, but by **selbst** or (in colloquial speech) **selber** placed at some point in the sentence after the noun or pronoun to which they refer (→**4**)

● **selbst/selber** do not change their form, regardless of number and gender of the noun to which they refer (→**4**)

● They are always stressed, regardless of their position in the sentence.

1 **Wir sind uns begegnet** We met (each other)
    Sie hatten sich auf einer Tagung kennengelernt
    They had got to know each other at a conference

2 **Wir kennen uns schon**
    OR:
    Wir kennen einander schon
    We already know each other

    Sie kennen sich schon
    OR:
    Sie kennen einander schon
    They already know each other

3 **Sie redeten miteinander**
    They were talking to each other

4 **Die Königin selbst hat es befohlen**
    The queen herself has given the order
    Ich habe es selbst nicht gelesen, aber ...
    I haven't read it myself, but ...

174 PRONOUNS

Relative Pronouns

These have the same forms as the definite article, except in the dative plural and genitive cases.

They are declined as follows:

| | singular | | | plural |
	masc	fem	neut	all genders
nom	der	die	das	die
acc	den	die	das	die
gen	dessen	deren	dessen	deren
dat	dem	der	dem	denen

- Relative pronouns must agree in gender and number with the noun to which they refer. They take their case however from the function they have in their own relative clause (→1)

- The relative pronoun cannot be omitted in German as it sometimes is in English (→2)

- The genitive forms are used in relative clauses in much the same way as in English (→3)
  Note however the translation of certain phrases (→4)

- When a preposition introduces the relative clause, the relative pronoun may be replaced by **wo-** or **wor-** if the noun or pronoun it stands for refers to an inanimate object or abstract concept (→5)
  The full form of relative pronoun plus preposition is however stylistically better.

- Relative clauses are always divided off by commas from the rest of the sentence (→1-5)

Continued

1 **Der Mann, den ich gestern gesehen habe, kommt aus Hamburg**
The man whom I saw yesterday comes from Hamburg

2 **Die Frau, mit der ich gestern gesprochen habe, kennt deine Mutter**
The woman I spoke to yesterday knows your mother

3 **Das Kind, dessen Fahrrad gestohlen worden war, ...**
The child whose bicycle had been stolen ...

4 **Die Kinder, von denen einige schon lesen konnten, ...**
The children, some of whom could read, ...
Meine Freunden, von denen einer ...
My friends, one of whom ...

5 **Der Zug, worauf wir warteten, hatte 20 Minuten Verspätung**
OR:
Der Zug, auf den wir warteten, hatte 20 MinutenVerspätung
The train we were waiting for was running 20 minutes late

Relative Pronouns (ctd.)

welcher

A second relative pronoun exists. This has the same forms as
the interrogative adjective **welcher** without the genitive
forms:

| | singular | | | plural |
	masc	fem	neut	all genders
nom	**welcher**	**welche**	**welches**	**welche**
acc	**welchen**	**welche**	**welches**	**welche**
gen	—	—	—	—
dat	**welchem**	**welcher**	**welchem**	**welchen**

● These forms are used only infrequently as relative
  pronouns, where sentence rhythm might benefit.

● They are also useful used as articles or adjectives to connect
  a noun in the relative clause with the contents of the main
  clause (→1)

wer, was

These are normally used as interrogative pronouns meaning
who?, *what?* and are declined as such on p.178.

● They may however also be used without interrogative
  meaning to replace both subject and relative pronoun in
  English:
  he who, a woman who, anyone who, those who etc (→2)

● **was** is the relative pronoun used in set expressions with
  certain neuter forms (→3)

1 **Er glaubte, mit der Hausarbeit nicht helfen zu brauchen,**
   mit welcher Idee seine Mutter nicht einverstanden war!
   He thought he didn't have to help in the house, an idea with
   which his mother was not in agreement!

2 **Wer das glaubt, ist verrückt**
   Anyone who believes that is mad
   Was mich angeht, ... For my part ...
   Was du gestern gekauft hast, steht dir ganz gut
   The things you bought yesterday suit you very well

3 **nichts, was ...** nothing that
   vieles, was... a lot that
   einiges, was ... some that
   dasselbe, was ... the same one that
   wenig, was ... little that
   dasjenige, was ... that which
   folgendes, was ... the following which
   manches, was ... some which
   allerlei, was ... all kinds of things that
   alles, was ... everything which
   das, was ... that which

   Nichts, was er sagte, hat gestimmt
   Nothing that he said was right
   Das, was du jetzt machst, ist reiner Unsinn!
   What you are doing now is sheer nonsense!
   Mit allem, was du mitgebracht hast, kommen wir gut aus
   We'll manage very well on everything that you've brought

Interrogative Pronouns

These are the pronouns used to ask questions.

As in English, they have few forms, singular and plural being the same.

They are declined as follows:

	persons	things
nom	**wer?**	**was?**
acc	**wen?**	**was?**
gen	**wessen?**	**wessen?**
dat	**wem?**	—

- They are used in direct questions (→1)
  or in indirect questions (→2)

- When used as the subject of a sentence, they are always followed by a singular verb (→3)
  EXCEPTION:
  When followed by a verb and taking a noun complement, the verb may be plural if the sense demands it (→4)

- The interrogative pronouns can be used in rhetorical questions or in exclamations (→5)

Continued

1 **Wer hat es gemacht?** Who did it?
   Mit wem bist du gekommen?
   Who did you come with?

2 **Ich weiß nicht, wer es gemacht hat**
   I don't know who did it
   Er wollte wissen, mit wem er fahren sollte
   He wanted to know who he was to travel with

3 **Wer kommt heute?** Who's coming today?

4 **Wer sind diese Leute?** Who are these people?

5 **Was haben wir gelacht!** How we laughed!

Interrogative Pronouns (ctd.)

● When used with prepositions, **was** usually becomes **wo-** and is placed in front of the preposition to form one word with it (→**1**)

Where the preposition begins with a vowel, **wor-** is used instead (→**2**)

This construction is similar to **da(r)-** + *preposition* shown on p.164

As with **da(r)-** + *preposition*, this construction is not used when the preposition is intended to convey movement. **Wohin** (*where to*) and **woher** (*where from*) are used instead (→**3**)

was für ein?, welcher?

● These are used to mean *what kind of one?* and *which one?*

● They are declined as shown on pp.124 and 128.

● They are used to form either direct or indirect questions (→**4**)

● They may refer either to persons or to things with the appropriate declension endings (→**5**)

1 Wo ist er? Where is he?
Er ist nicht da He isn't there

Hier darf man nicht parken
You can't park here

2 Klaus und Ulli geben heute eine Party. Gehen wir hin?
Klaus and Ulli are giving a party today. Shall we go?

3 Wohin fährst du? Where are you going?

Sie liefen überallhin They ran everywhere

4 Woher kommst du? Where do you come from?

Woher hast du das? Where did you get that from?

Das habe ich irgendwoher gekriegt
I got that from somewhere or other

Comparison of Adverbs

- The **comparative** form of the adverb is obtained in exactly the same way as that of adjectives, i.e. by adding **-er** (→1)

- The **superlative** form is formed as follows:
  am + *adverb* + **-sten/-esten**
  It is not declined (→2)

- Note the use of the comparative adverb with **immer** to show progression (→3)

- *the more ... the more ...* is expressed in German by **je ... desto ...** or **je ... um so ...** (→4)

- Some adverbial superlatives are used to show the extent of a quality rather than a comparison with others. These are as follows:
  spätestens *at the latest*
  höchstens *at the most; at best*
  wenigstens *at least*
  meistens *mostly; most often*
  strengstens *strictly, absolutely*
  bestens *very well; very warmly* (→5)

- Two irregular comparatives and superlatives:
  gern → lieber → am liebsten (used with **haben**)
  well → better → best

  bald → eher → am ehesten
  soon → sooner → soonest (→6)

1 **Er läuft schneller als seine Schwester**
   He runs faster than his sister

   Ich sehe ihn seltener als früher
   I see him less often than before

2 **Wer von ihnen arbeitet am schnellsten?**
   Which of them works fastest?

   Er ißt am meisten He eats most

3 **Die Mädchen sprachen immer lauter**
   The girls were talking more and more loudly

   Er fuhr immer langsamer
   He drove more and more slowly

4 **Je eher, desto besser** The sooner the better

5 **Er kommt meistens zu spät an**
   He usually arrives late

   Rauchen strengstens verboten!
   No smoking

6 **Welches hast du am liebsten?**
   Which do you like best?

Emphasizers

These are words commonly used in German, as indeed in English, especially in the spoken language, to emphasize or modify in some way the meaning of the sentence. The following are some of the most common:

aber
Used to lend emphasis to a statement (→1)

denn
As well as its uses as a conjunction (see p.214), **denn** is widely used to emphasize the meaning. It often cannot be directly translated (→2)

doch
Is used as a positive reply in order to correct negative assumptions or impressions (→3)

It can strengthen an imperative (→4)

It can make a question out of a statement (→5)

mal
May be used with imperatives (→6)

It also has several idiomatic uses (→7)

ja
Strengthens a statement (→8)

It also has several idiomatic uses (→9)

schon
Is used familiarly with an imperative (→10)

It is also used in various idiomatic ways (→11)

1 Das ist aber schön! Oh that's pretty!
  Aber doch! Yes indeed!

2 Was ist denn hier los?
  What's going on here then?
  Wo denn? Where?

3 Hat es dir nicht gefallen? — Doch!
  Didn't you like it? — Oh yes, I did!

4 Laß ihn doch! Just leave him

5 Das schaffst du doch!
  You'll manage it, won't you?

6 Komm mal her! Come here!
  Moment mal! Just a minute!

7 Mal sehen We'll see
  Er soll es nur mal versuchen!
  Just let him try it!
  Hören Sie mal ... Look here now ...

8 Er sieht ja wie seine Mutter aus
  He looks like his mother
  Das kann ja sein That may well be

9 Ja und? So what?/What then?
  Das ist ja lächerlich That's ridiculous
  Das ist es ja That's just it

10 Laß schon! Let it be!/Leave it alone!

11 Wenn schon! What of it?/So what?
  Schon gut Okay /Very well

Prepositions

In English, a preposition does not affect the word or phrase which it introduces e.g.

the women / a large meal / these events
with the women / *after* a large meal / *before* these events

In German, however, the noun following a preposition must be put in a certain *case*:
accusative   ($\rightarrow$**1**)
dative   ($\rightarrow$**2**)
genitive   ($\rightarrow$**3**)

It is therefore important to learn each preposition with the case, or cases, it governs.

The following guidelines will help you:

- Prepositions which take the accusative or dative cases are much more common than those taking the genitive case.

- Certain prepositions may take a dative or accusative case, depending on whether *movement* is involved or not. This is explained further on pp.202 ff. ($\rightarrow$**4**)

- Prepositions are often used to complete the sense of certain verbs, as shown on p.76ff ($\rightarrow$**5**)

- After many prepositions, a shortened or *contracted* form of the definite article may be merged with the preposition to form one word, e.g.

auf + das	becomes **aufs**
bei + dem	becomes **beim**
zu + der	becomes **zur**

Continued

1 **Es ist für dich**
It's for you
Wir sind durch die ganze Welt gereist
We travelled all over the world

2 **Er ist mit seiner Frau gekommen**
He came with his wife

3 **Es ist ihm trotz seiner Bemühungen mißlungen**
Despite his efforts, he still didn't succeed

4 **Es liegt auf dem Tisch**
It's on the table (*dative*: no movement implied)
Lege es bitte auf den Tisch Please put it on the table
(*accusative*: movement *onto* the table)

5 **Ich warte auf meinen Mann**
I'm waiting for my husband

Prepositions: contracted forms (ctd.)

Such contractions are possible with the following prepositions:

preposition	+ das	+ den	+ dem	+ der
hinter	hinters*	hintern*	hinterm*	
über	übers*	übern*	überm*	
unter	unters*	untern*	unterm*	
zu			zum	zur
an	ans		am	
vor	vors*		vorm*	
in	ins		im	
bei			beim	
von			vom	
durch	durchs*			
für	fürs*			
auf	aufs*			
um	ums*			

- Those forms marked with an asterisk are suitable only for use in colloquial, spoken German.
  All other forms (not marked with an asterisk) may be safely used in any context, formal or informal (→1)

- Contracted forms are obviously not used where the article is to be stressed (→2)

- Other contracted forms involving prepositions, as shown on p.164 and 174, occur:
  1) in the introduction to relative clauses (→3)
  2) with personal pronouns representing inanimate objects (→4)

Continued

1 Wir gehen heute Abend ins Theater
We are going to the theatre this evening

Er geht zur Schule
He goes to school

Das kommt vom Trinken
That comes from drinking

2 In die Schule geht mein Sohn aber nicht!
My son is certainly not going to that school!

3 Die Bank, worauf wir saßen, war etwas wackelig
The bench we were sitting on was somewhat wobbly

4 Er war damit zufrieden
He was satisfied with that

Er hat es darauf gesetzt
He put it on it

Prepositions followed by the Dative Case

Some of the most common prepositions taking the dative case are:

aus	**gegenüber**	**seit**
außer	**mit**	**von**
bei	**nach**	**zu**

aus
- as a preposition meaning *out of/from* (→**1**)

- as a separable verbal prefix (see p.72) (→**2**)

außer
- as a preposition meaning: *out of* (→**3**)

  except (→**4**)

bei
- as a preposition meaning: *at the home/shop/work (etc) of* (→**5**)

  near (→**6**)

  in the course of/during (→**7**)

- as a separable verbal prefix (see p.72) (→**8**)

gegenüber
- as a preposition meaning: *opposite* (→**9**)

  to(wards) (→**10**)

  NOTE: when used as a preposition, **gegenüber** is placed *after a pronoun*, but may be placed *before or after a noun*

- as a separable verbal prefix (→**11**)

Continued

1 durch das Fenster blicken
to look through the window

2 Durch seine Bemühungen wurden alle gerettet
Everyone was saved through his efforts

3 die Straße entlang
along the street

4 die Straße entlanggehen
to go along the street

5 Ich habe es für dich getan
I did it for you

6 Das ist für ihn sehr wichtig
That is very important to him

7 Was für Äpfel sind das?
What kind of apples are they?

8 Stelle es gegen die Mauer
Put it against the wall
Haben Sie ein Mittel gegen Schnupfen?
Have you something for (= against) colds?
Ich habe nichts dagegen
I've got nothing against it

9 Wir sind gegen vier angekommen
We arrived around/at getting on for four o'clock

Prepositions followed by the Accusative Case (ctd.)

ohne

- as a preposition meaning *without* (→**1**)

um

- as a preposition meaning: (a)*round/round about* (→**2**)

  at (in time expressions) (→**3**)

  for (after certain verbs) (→**4**)

  about (after certain verbs) (→**5**)

  by (in expressions of quantity) (→**6**)

- as a variable verbal prefix (see p.74) (→**7**)

wider

- as a preposition meaning *contrary to/against* (→**8**)

- as a variable verbal prefix (see p.74) (→**9**)

Continued

1 Ohne ihn geht's nicht
It won't work without him

2 um die Ecke (a)round the corner

3 Es fängt um neun Uhr an It begins at nine

4 Sie baten ihre Mutter um Kekse
They asked their mother for some biscuits

5 Es handelt sich um dein Benehmen
It's a question of your behaviour

6 Es ist um zehn Mark billiger
It is cheaper by ten marks

7 umarmen to embrace (*inseparable*) →
Er hat sie umarmt
He gave her a hug

umfallen to fall over (*separable*) →
Er ist umgefallen
He fell over

8 Das geht mir wider die Natur
That's against my nature

9 widersprechen to go against (*inseparable*) →
Das hat meinen Wünschen widersprochen
That went against my wishes

widertönen to echo (*separable*) →
Seine Worte tönte ihr noch im Ohr wider
His words were still ringing in her ears

Prepositions followed by the Dative or the Accusative

These prepositions are followed by:

the **accusative** when *movement towards* a different place is involved

the **dative** when *position* is described as opposed to movement, or when the movement is *within* the same place.

- The most common prepositions in this category are:

  in *in/into/to* (→1)
  an *on/at/to*
  auf *on/in/to/at*
  unter *under/among* (→2)
  über *over/across/above*
  vor *in front of/before*
  hinter *behind*
  neben *next to/beside*
  zwischen *between* (→3)

- These prepositions may also be used with figurative meanings as part of a *verb + preposition* construction (see p.76).
  The case following **auf** or **an** is then not the same after all verbs (→4)
  It is therefore best to learn such constructions together with the case which follows them.

- Many of these prepositions are also used as verb prefixes in the same way as the prepositions described on pp.202 to 209 (→5)

Continued

1   **Er ging ins Zimmer** (*acc*)
He entered the room

    Im Zimmer (*dat*) **warteten viele Leute auf ihn**
A lot of people were waiting for him in the room

2   **Er rannte unter das Dach** (*acc*)
He ran in under the roof

    Er lebte dort unter Freunden (*dat*)
There he lived among friends

3   **Er legte es zwischen die beiden Teller** (*acc*)
He put it between the two plates

    Das Dorf liegt zwischen den Bergen (*dat*)
The village lies between the mountains

4   **sich verlassen auf** (+ *acc*) to depend on
    bestehen auf (+ *dat*) to insist on

    glauben an (+ *acc*) to believe in
    leiden an (+ *dat*) to suffer from

5   **anrechnen** to charge for (*separable*) →
    Das wird Ihnen später angerechnet
You'll be charged for that later

    aufsetzen to put on (*separable*) →
    Sie setzte sich den Hut auf
She put her hat on

    überqueren to cross (*inseparable*) →
    Sie hat die Straße überquert
She crossed the street

Prepositions followed by the Genitive Case

The following are some of the more common prepositions which take the genitive case:

diesseits *on this side of*
jenseits *on the other side of* (→1)
beiderseits *on both sides of*
innerhalb *within/inside* (→2)
außerhalb *outside*
während* *during* (→3)
statt* *instead of*
trotz* *in spite of* (→4)
wegen* *on account of* (→5)
infolge *as a result of*
hinsichtlich *with regard to*
... halber *for ... sake/because of ...*
um ... willen *for ... sake/because of ...*

- Those prepositions marked with an asterisk may also be followed by the dative case (→6)

- Note that special forms of the possessive and relative pronouns are used with **wegen, halber** and **willen** (→7)

1 jenseits der Grenze
on the other side of the frontier

2 innerhalb dieses Zeitraums
within this period of time

3 während der Vorstellung
during the performance

4 trotz seiner Befürchtungen
despite his apprehensions

5 wegen der neuen Stelle
because of the new job

6 trotz allem in spite of everything
wegen mir because of me

7 meinetwegen on my account, because of me
deinetwegen on your account, because of you
seinetwegen on his account, because of him
ihretwegen on her/their account, because of her/them
unsertwegen on our account, because of us
euertwegen on your account, because of you
Ihretwegen on your account, because of you (*polite*)
derentwegen for whose sake, for her/their/its sake
dessentwegen for whose sake, for his/its sake

meinethalben *etc* on my *etc* account
derenthalben on whose account, on her/their/its account
dessenthalben on whose account, on his/its account

meinetwillen *etc* for my *etc* sake
derentwillen for whose sake, for her/its/their sake
dessentwillen for whose sake, for his/its sake

Co-ordinating Conjunctions

These are used to link words, phrases or clauses (→1)

● These are the main co-ordinating conjunctions:

    und and (→1)

    oder or (→2)

    aber but (→3)
            however (→4)

    denn for (→5)

    sondern but (after a negative construction) (→6)

● These do not cause subject-verb inversion, i.e. the verb follows the subject in the normal way (see p.224) (→1-6)

● Inversion may however be caused by something other than the co-ordinating conjunction, e.g. **dann, trotzdem, montags** in the examples opposite (→7)

● When used with the meaning of *however*, **aber** is placed within the clause, and not at the beginning (→4)

● When linked by co-ordinating conjunctions, no comma is required between clauses (cf. p.240).

Continued

1 **Peter und Veronika** Peter and Veronika
   Er ging in die Stadt und kaufte sich ein neues Hemd
   He went into town and bought himself a new shirt

2 **Er hatte noch nie Whisky oder Schnaps getrunken**
   He had never drunk whisky or schnapps
   Willst du eins, oder hast du vielleicht keinen Hunger?
   Do you want one or aren't you hungry?

3 **Wir wollten ins Kino, aber wir hatten kein Geld**
   We wanted to go to the cinema but we had no money

4 **Ich wollte ins Theater; er aber wollte nicht mit**
   I wanted to go to the theatre; however he wouldn't come

5 **Wir wollten heute fahren, denn montags ist weniger Verkehr**
   We wanted to travel today because the traffic is lighter on
   Mondays

6 **Er ist nicht alt, sondern jung**
   He isn't old, but young

7 **Er hat sie besucht, und dann ist er wieder nach Hause
   gegangen**
   He paid her a visit and then went home again
   **Wir wollten doch ins Kino, aber trotzdem sind wir zu Hause
   geblieben**
   We wanted to go to the cinema, but even so stayed at home
   Wir wollten heute fahren, denn montags ist weniger Verkehr
   We wanted to travel today, because there is less traffic on
   Mondays

Double Co-ordinating Conjunctions

These conjunctions consist of two separate elements, like their English counterparts e.g.

> *not only ... but also ...*

The following are widely used:

sowohl ... als (auch) *both ... and*

- This may link words or phrases (→**1**)

- The verb is usually plural, whether the subjects are singular or plural (→**1**)

weder ... noch *neither ... nor*

- This may link words or phrases (→**2**)

- It may also link clauses, and inversion of subject and verb then takes place in both clauses (→**3**)

- The verb is plural unless both subjects are singular (→**4**)

Continued

1 **Sowohl sein Vater als auch seine Mutter haben sich darüber gefreut**
Both his father and his mother were pleased about it

Sowohl unser Lehrkörper als auch unsere Schüler haben teilgenommen
Both our staff and our pupils took part

2 **Weder Georg noch sein Bruder kannte das Mädchen**
Neither George nor his brother knew the girl

3 **Weder mag ich ihn, noch respektiere ich ihn**
I neither like nor respect him

4 **Weder die Damen noch die Herren haben recht**
Neither the ladies nor the gentlemen are right

Weder du noch ich würde es schaffen
Neither you nor I would be able to do it

Double Co-ordinating Conjunctions (ctd.)

nicht nur ... sondern auch *not only ... but also*

- This is used to link clauses as well as words and phrases (→1)

- The word order is: inversion of subject and verb in the first clause, and normal order in the second (→2)
  However, if **nicht nur** does not begin the clause, normal order prevails (→3)

- The verb agrees in number with the subject nearest to it (→4)

entweder ... oder *either ... or*

- The verb agrees with the subject nearest it (→5)

- The normal word order is: inversion in the first clause, and normal order in the second (→6)
  However, it is possible to use normal order in the first clause, and this lends a threatening tone to the statement (→7)

teils ... teils *partly ... partly*

- The verb is normally plural unless both subjects are singular (→8)

- Inversion of subject and verb takes place in both clauses (→9)

1 **Er ist nicht nur geschickt, sondern auch intelligent**
Nicht nur ist er geschickt, sondern er ist auch intelligent
He is not only skilful but also intelligent

2 **Nicht nur hat es die ganze Zeit geregnet, sondern ich habe**
mir auch noch das Bein gebrochen
Not only did it rain the whole time, but I also broke my leg

3 **Es hat nicht nur die ganze Zeit geregnet, sondern ich habe**
mir auch noch das Bein gebrochen
Not only did it rain the whole time, but I also broke my leg

4 **Nicht nur ich, sondern auch die Mädchen sind dafür**
verantwortlich
Not just me, but the girls too are responsible
Nicht nur sie, sondern auch hat es gehört
It wasn't only they who heard it — I heard it too

5 **Entweder du oder Georg muß es getan haben**
It must have been either you or George who did it

6 **Entweder komme ich morgen vorbei, oder ich ruf dich an**
I'll either drop in tomorrow or I'll give you a ring

7 **Entweder du gibst das sofort auf, oder du kriegst kein**
Taschengeld mehr
Either you give it up immediately, or you get no more pocket
money

8 **Die Studenten waren teils Deutsche, teils Ausländer**
The students were partly German and partly from abroad

9 **Teils bin ich überzeugt, teils bleib ich skeptisch**
A bit of me is convinced, and a bit remains sceptical

Subordinating Conjunctions

These are used to link clauses in such a way as to make one clause dependent on another for its meaning. The dependent clause is called a **subordinate clause** and the other a **main clause**.

● The subordinate clause is always separated from the rest of the sentence by commas (→1)

● The subordinate clause may precede the main clause. When this happens, the verb and subject of the main clause are inverted i.e. they swap places, as shown on p.226 (→2)

● The finite part of the verb (i.e. the conjugated part) is always at the end of a subordinate clause (see p.228) (→3)

● For compound tenses in subordinate clauses, it is the **auxiliary** (the main part of the verb) which comes last, after the participle or infinitive used to form the compound tense (see the section on compound tenses) (→4)

● Any **modal verb (mögen, können** etc. — p.52ff) used in a subordinate clause is placed last in the clause (→5)

EXCEPTION : when the modal verb is in a compound tense, the order is as shown (→6)

Continued

1 Seine Mutter trinkt Whisky
His mother drinks whisky

2 Sie wird dir etwas sagen She will tell you something
Sie hat mir nichts gesagt She told me nothing
Es ist für ihn gekauft worden It was bought for him

1	2
3 Die neuen Waren	**kommen morgen**
The new goods	are coming tomorrow

1	2
Was du gesagt hast,	**stimmt nicht**
What you said	isn't true

4 Er rasierte sich He shaved
Er hat sich rasiert He (has) shaved

5 ein alter Mann an old man
diese alten Sachen these old things

6 Ich gab dem Mann das Geld I gave the man the money
Ich gab ihm das Geld I gave him the money
Ich gab es ihm I gave him it/I gave it to him
Ich gab es dem Mann I gave it to the man
Er gab das Geld seiner Schwester
He gave the money to his sister (*not his brother*)

7 Gestern gingen wir ins Theater ⎫ We went to the theatre
Wir gingen gestern ins Theater ⎭ yesterday

8 Dort haben sie Fußball gespielt ⎫ They played football
Sie haben dort Fußball gespielt ⎭ there

9 Sie spielen gut Fußball They play football well
Das war furchtbar teuer It was terribly expensive

10 Sie haben gestern furchtbar schlecht dort gespielt
They played dreadfully badly there yesterday

Word Order: Main Clauses (ctd.)

- A pronoun object precedes all adverbs (→1)
- While the main verb must normally remain the second concept, the first concept need not always be the subject. Main clauses can begin with many things, including:
  - an adverb (→2)
  - a direct or indirect object (→3)
  - an infinitive phrase (→4)
  - a complement (→5)
  - a past participle (→6)
  - a prepositional phrase (→7)
  - a clause acting as the object of the verb (→8)
  - a subordinate clause (→9)
- If the subject does not begin a main clause, the verb and subject must be turned around or "inverted" (→2-9)
- Beginning a sentence with something other than the subject is frequent in German.
  It may however also be used for special effect to:
  highlight whatever is placed first in the clause (→10)
  emphasize the subject of the clause by forcing it from its initial position to the end of the clause (→11)
- After inversion, any reflexive pronoun precedes the subject, unless the subject is a pronoun (→12)
- The following do not cause inversion when placed at the beginning of a main clause, although inversion may be caused by something else placed after them:
  und, allein, oder, sondern, denn (→13)
  ja and **nein** (→14)
  certain exclamations: **ach, also, nun** *etc* (→15)
  words or phrases qualifying the subject: **nur, sogar, auch** *etc* (→16)

1 Sie haben es gestern sehr billig gekauft
  They bought it very cheaply yesterday
2 Gestern sind wir ins Theater gegangen
  We went to the theatre yesterday
3 So ein Kind habe ich noch nie gesehen! I've never seen such a child!
  Seinen Freunden wollte er aber nicht helfen
  He wouldn't help his friends
4 Seinen Freunden zu helfen, hat er nicht versucht
  He didn't try to help his friends
5 Deine Schwester war es It was your sister
6 Geraucht hatte er nie He had never smoked
7 In diesem Haus ist Mozart auf die Welt gekommen
  Mozart was born in this house
8 Was mit ihm los war, haben wir nicht herausgefunden
  We never discovered what was wrong with him
9 Nachdem ich ihn gesehen hatte, ging ich nach Hause
  I went home after seeing him
10 Dem würde ich nichts sagen! I wouldn't tell *him* anything
11 An der Ecke stand eine riesengroße Fabrik
  A huge factory stood on the corner
12 Daran erinnerten sich die Zeugen nicht
  The witnesses didn't remember that
  Daran erinnerten sie sich nicht They didn't remember that
13 Peter ging nach Hause, und Elsa blieb auf der Party
  Peter went home and Elsa stayed at the party
  BUT **Peter ging nach Hause, und unterwegs sah er Kurt**
    Peter went home and on the way he saw Kurt
14 Nein, ich will nicht No, I don't want to
  BUT **Nein, das tue ich nicht** No I won't do that
15 Also, wir fahren nach Hamburg So we'll go to Hamburg
  BUT **Also, nach Hamburg wollt ihr fahren**
    So you want to go to Hamburg
16 Nur seine Mutter wollte es ihm nicht glauben
  Only his mother wouldn't believe him
  BUT **Sogar mit dem Zug ginge es nicht schneller**
    It would be no faster even by train

Word Order: Subordinate Clauses

- A subordinate clause may be introduced by:
    a relative pronoun (see p.174) (→1)
    a subordinating conjunction (see p.222) (→2-3)

- The subject follows the opening conjunction or relative pronoun — **wir** and **er** in examples **1-3**

- The main verb almost always goes to the end of a subordinate clause (→1-3)

    The exceptions to this are:

    1. in a **wenn** clause where **wenn** is omitted (see p.64) (→4)
    2. in an indirect statement without **daß** (see p. 64) (→5)

- The order for articles, nouns, adjectives, adverbs, direct and indirect objects is the same as for main clauses (see p. 224), but they are all placed between the subject of the clause and the verb (→6)

- If the subject of a reflexive verb in a subordinate clause is a pronoun, the order is *subject pronoun + reflexive pronoun* (→7) If the subject is a noun, the reflexive pronoun may follow or precede it (→8)

- Where one subordinate clause lies inside another, both still obey the order rule for subordinate clauses (→9)

1 **Die Kinder, die wir gesehen haben ...**
The children whom we saw ...

2 **Da er nicht schwimmen wollte, ist er nicht mitgekommen**
As he didn't want to swim he didn't come

3 **Ich weiß, daß er zur Zeit in London wohnt**
I know he's living in London at the moment
Ich weiß nicht, ob er kommt
I don't know if he's coming

4 **Findest du meine Uhr, so ruf mich bitte an**
(= Wenn du meine Uhr findest, ruf mich bitte an)
If you find my watch, please give me a ring

5 **Er meint, er werde es innerhalb einer Stunde schaffen**
(= Er meint, daß er es innerhalb einer Stunde schaffen
werde)
He thinks (that) he would manage it inside an hour

6 *main clause:*
Er ist gestern mit seiner Mutter in die Stadt gefahren
He went to town with his mother yesterday
subordinate clauses:
Da er gestern mit seiner Mutter in die Stadt gefahren ist ...
Since he went to town with his mother yesterday ...
Der Junge, der gestern mit seiner Mutter in die Stadt
gefahren ist ...
The boy who went to town with his mother yesterday
Ich weiß, daß er gestern mit seiner Mutter in die Stadt
gefahren ist
I know that he went to town with his mother yesterday

7 **Weil er sich nicht setzen wollte ...**
Because he wouldn't sit down ...

8 **Weil das Kind sich nicht setzen wollte, ...**
OR: **Weil sich das Kind nicht setzen wollte, ...**
because the child wouldn't sit down

9 **Er wußte, daß der Mann, mit dem er früher gesprochen**
hatte, bei einer Baufirma arbeitete
He knew that the man he had been speaking to earlier worked
for a construction company

Word Order (ctd.)

In The Imperative

- normal order (→**1**)

- with reflexive verbs (→**2**)

- with separable verbs (→**3**)

- with separable reflexive verbs (→**4**)

In Direct and Indirect speech

- the verb of saying ("he replied/he said") must be inverted if it is placed within a quotation (→**5**)

- the position of the verb in indirect speech depends on whether or not **daß** (see p.66) is used (→**6**)

Verbs with Separable Prefixes (see p.72 to 75)

- in main clauses the verb and prefix are separated in simple tenses and imperative forms (→**7**)

- for compound tenses of main clauses and all tenses of subordinate clauses, the verb and its prefix are united at the end of the clause (→**8**)

- in a present infinitive phrase (see p.46), the verb and prefix are joined together by **zu** and placed at the end of the phrase (→**9**)

1   **Hol mir das Buch!** (*singular*)
   Holt mir das Buch! (*plural*)   } Fetch me that book!
   Holen Sie mir das Buch! (*polite*)

2   **Wasch dich Sofort!**   Wash yourself at once!
   Wascht euch Sofort!   Wash yourselves at once!
   Waschen Sie sich sofort! (*polite*)

3   **Hör jetzt auf!** (*singular*)
   Hört jetzt auf! (*plural*)   } Stop it!
   Hören Sie jetzt auf! (*polite*)

4   **Dreh dich um!** (*singular*)
   Dreh euch um! (*plural*)   } Turn round!
   Drehen Sie sich um! (*polite*)

5   **"Meine Mutter"** sagte er, **"kommt erst morgen an"**
   "My mother," he said, "won't arrive till tomorrow"

6   **Er sagte, daß sie erst am nächsten Tag ankomme**
   He said that she would not arrive until the next day
   Er sagte, sie komme erst am nächsten Tag an
   He said she would not arrive until the next day

7   **Er machte die Tür zu** He closed the door
   Ich räume zuerst auf I'll clean up first
   Hol mich um 7 ab! Pick me up at 7 o'clock!

8   **Er hat die Tür zugemacht** He closed the door
   Ich werde zuerst aufräumen I'll clean up first
   Er wurde um 7 abgeholt He was picked up at 7
   Wenn du mich um 7 abholst, ... If you pick me up at 7
   Nachdem du mich abgeholt hast, ...
   After you've picked me up

9   **Um frühzeitig anzukommen, fuhren wir sofort ab**
   In order to arrive early we left immediately

Question Forms

Direct Questions

- In German, a direct question is formed by simply inverting the verb and subject (→**1**)

- In compound tenses (see pp.22ff), the past participle or infinitive goes to the end of the clause (→**2**)

- A statement can be made into a question by the addition of **nicht, nicht wahr** or **doch**, as with "isn't it" in English (→**3**)
  Questions formed in this way normally expect the answer to be "yes".

- When a question is put in the negative, **doch** can be used to answer it more positively than **ja** (→**4**)

Questions Formed Using Interrogative Words

- When questions are formed with **interrogative adverbs**, the subject and verb are inverted (→**5**)

- When questions are formed with **interrogative pronouns** and **adjectives** (see p.144 and 176 to 178), the word order is that of direct statements:
  1. as the subject of the verb at the beginning of the clause they do not cause inversion (→**6**)
  2. if *not* the subject of the verb *and* at the beginning of the clause they do cause inversion (→**7**)

Indirect Questions

These are questions following verbs of asking and wondering *etc.* The verb comes at the end of an indirect question (→**8**)

INDEX **247**